THE VOICE IN CINEMA

THE VOICE IN CINEMA

Michel Chion

Edited and translated by Claudia Gorbman

COLUMBIA UNIVERSITY PRESS
NEW YORK

Columbia University Press wishes to express its appreciation of assistance given by the government of France through Le Ministère de la Culture in the preparation of the translation.

COLUMBIA UNIVERSITY PRESS

New York

Columbia University Press

Publishers Since 1893

New York   Chichester, West Sussex

Library of Congress Cataloging-in-Publication Data

Chion, Michel, 1947–

  [Voix au cinéma. English]

  The voice in cinema / Michel Chion ; edited and translated by

Claudia Gorbman.

    p. cm.

  Includes bibliographical references and index.

  ISBN 0–231–10822–2 (alk. paper). — ISBN 0–231–10823–0 (pbk.)

  1. Voice in motion pictures. 2. Motion pictures—Aesthetics.

3. Voice-overs. I. Gorbman, Claudia. II. Title.

PN1995.C4713 1999

791.43′02′908—dc21   98–19048

Casebound editions of Columbia University Press books are printed on permanent and durable acid-free paper.

Printed in the United States of America

Designed by Linda Secondari

c 10 9 8 7 6 5 4 3 2 1

p 10 9 8 7 6 5 4 3 2 1

To Christiane Sacco

CONTENTS

AUTHOR'S NOTE

The films and filmmakers chosen as examples in this book reflect the author's tastes. Readers may easily find in their own memories a thousand films to serve equally well. This is neither a history nor an anthology, but rather an outline for a theory of the film as sound film.

That I am considering primarily the *speaking* voice—the tenth chapter stops at the frontier of the *singing* voice—it's because I have reserved everything that has to do with music and the singing voice for another book, yet to be written.

The progression of this book is not linear. Its three sections, following an introductory chapter, are basically independent. The last two sections, however, are complementary. Taking Fritz Lang's Mabuse as emblematic, the first part considers the hidden, faceless voice and its magical powers, the myth of the *Acousmêtre*. Figured in *Psycho*'s Norman, the impossible or monstrous marriage of the filmed voice and body—the myth of the *Anacousmêtre*—is the subject of the third section. Between these two figures, the former masculine and the latter androgynous, comes the figure of the Mother in Mizoguchi's *Sansho the Bailiff*, Tamaki, under the rubric of which you will find five separate chapters as *"Tales of the Voice in Cinema"*; here there are essays on entrapment by telephone, voice-thieves, screams of terror, siren calls, and the silence of mute characters.

Two films return again and again throughout these pages: Alfred Hitchcock's *Psycho* and Fritz Lang's *Testament of Dr. Mabuse*. I see Lang's film, which appeared at the dawn of the sound era, as a sort of template for the voice in cinema.

I would like to thank for their help the editing, administration, and production staffs of *Cahiers du cinéma*, and also the staff, faculty and students of the IDHEC film school (Institut des Hautes Etudes Cinématographiques) and the DERCAV, the film and media department at the University of Paris III.

M.C.

EDITOR'S NOTE

La Voix au cinéma appeared in 1982 in a critical milieu very different from our own. France's artistic and intellectual climate of the late 1970s was suffused with "theory." The presence of three forces was particularly felt: Lacanian and Freudian psychoanalysis as they revolutionized literary and film studies, French feminism and its investigation of the gendered structure of language, and the cinematic/narrative experiments of Marguerite Duras. All three discourses gave prominence to the voice in different ways, allowing Michel Chion to open his book with the observation that "the voice is in the air."

A combination of poet and keen observer/listener, as well as an admirer of Lacan, Chion here presents a work that is less theoretical than imaginative, drawing insights from films and theory in the air.

It is difficult to think of films and their evolution in quite the same way after reading Chion. Of course, we say, the voice is central to the cinema as we know it. At least, we say, after *The Jazz Singer* and the subsequent domination of the cinema by the human voice. What about the voice? Of course, we say, it is speech, and song, that organize movies, and then we focus attention on the words (or less often, the musical qualities of songs) that fall from the shadows of mouths we see on the screen. But it is the voice—not as speech, not as song, but everything that's left afterward, that is the subject of Chion's investigation.

The cinema's deployment of the human voice, the special relationships that inhere between the voice and the cinematic image, gendered voices in films, screams, the absence of voices, and technologies of the voice in what itself is a technological medium, constitute the terrain for this book. Chion reflects on the voice as an absolutely central, though much ignored, feature of sound films.

Since the late 1920s popular and independent movies alike continue to revolve around the voice, constantly reinventing its possibilities. The landscape to explore includes the rhythms and textures of rap, the distinctive voices of Robin Williams and Fran Drescher and James Earl Jones, the digitally synthesized voices of villainous and heroic cyborgs, the telephone voice and the cellular phone, muteness (a throwback to silent film?), actors who are chameleons with their voices (Brando, De Niro), and those stars whose voices are constant (Schwarzenegger, Bruce Willis).

Chion tackles his subject with a certain egalitarian fervor. In a single paragraph he might consider Peter Greenaway and *Look Who's Talking*. It's not that he ever confuses the popular cinema with the art cinema, but he considers both equally likely to advance cinematic language, to innovate terms of film "vocabulary," to confront the challenges and opportunities of technological developments, and forge new kinds of expression from them.

La Voix au cinéma helped to establish Michel Chion's reputation as a major voice in France. Americans, with very few exceptions, are far less familiar with this work than with that of Christian Metz, Raymond Bellour, or Michel Marie, all of whom had distinguished academic reputations and major posts in universities and institutes. Chion's career has straddled the two realms of creation and criticism: he is a reputed composer of *musique concrète*, and a sometime filmmaker, as well as a writer of some twenty books to date (translated into a wide variety of languages).

His use of the theoretical models he invokes is far less rigorous than those of the "purer" academics. Unlike Metz, for example, whose applications of theory to actual film analysis is relatively limited, Chion begins with specific film phenomena and draws insights from there. It is perhaps this critical stance rooted firmly in practice, both as an artist himself and a critic for *Cahiers du cinéma* and other periodicals, that helps explain in part the slow awakening of American film studies to Chion's contributions. His essays vibrate with original thought. Even Kaja Silverman, who in *The Acoustic Mirror* (1987) sets him up as her non-feminist straw man, heaps praise in a footnote on his reading of *Citizen Kane*. The writing abounds with neologisms, in Chion's restless search for concepts adequate to a subject that has not been sufficiently mapped—which, indeed, seems stubbornly resistant to film scholarship: constantly touched upon, then bypassed or short-circuited.

The author has decided in most cases to preserve the original introduction and ten chapters as printed in the 1982 text. For this edition he has added a closing chapter in order to give the book fuller relevance for the late 1990s, recognizing trends in film style, technology, and content that have enriched the subject of the cinematic voice in the last fifteen years. As we spent a few days in Paris in the summer of 1997 discussing what should go into this last chapter, it became clear to me how much passion—and ruthless self-editing—routinely go into Chion's work. This explains the compactness of *The Voice in Cinema* and, it is hoped, its productive richness.

THE VOICE IN CINEMA

Karl Meixner in Fritz Lang's
Testament of Dr. Mabuse
(1932).

PROLOGUE RAISING THE VOICE

STRANGE OBJECT   The voice is elusive. Once you've eliminated everything that is not the voice itself—the body that houses it, the words it carries, the notes it sings, the traits by which it defines a speaking person, and the timbres that color it, what's left? What a strange object, what grist for poetic outpourings . . . I say this because French writing on the voice these days seems like so much formless verbalizing, resolutely skirting the clear and systematic language necessary for making headway.

How can we think about the voice? Freudian psychoanalysis, invented in the form of a talking cure, could have seized upon the voice as an object of study, for in psychoanalysis everything happens *in* and *through* speech, even if it only uses the voice as a vehicle for the verbal signifier. But a serious theoretical elaboration of the voice as an object did become possible with Lacan, when he placed the voice—along with the gaze, the penis, the feces, and nothingness—in the ranks of *"objet (a),"* these *part objects* which may be fetishized and employed to "thingify difference."[1] And building on Lacan, the excellent book by Denis Vasse, *L'Ombilic et la voix* (*The Umbilicus and the Voice*, published in 1974), proposed one of the first consistent and dialectical approaches to the topic. Vasse's work allowed us not only to speak "around" the voice, but also to consider it as an object, without either becoming lost in the fascination it inspires or reducing it to being merely the vehicle of language and expression.

THERE IS NO SOUNDTRACK   By what incomprehensible thoughtlessness can we, in considering what after all is called the talking picture, "forget" the voice? Because we confuse it with speech. From the speech act we usually retain only the significations it bears, forgetting the medium of the voice itself. Of course the voice is there to be forgotten in its materiality; only at this cost does it fill its primary function.

1. Cf. for example Jacques Lacan, *Ecrits* (Paris: Editions du Seuil, 1966), p. 817; Lacan, *Ecrits: A Selection*, Alan Sheridan, trans. (London: Tavistock, 1977), pp. 314–15. "Objets petit autres": objects with only a little otherness, objects the child previously experienced as parts of itself. See Alan Sheridan's translation in Jacques Lacan, *Ecrits: A Selection* (London: Tavistock, 1977), pp. 314–315.

I

Greta Garbo being directed by Jacques Feyder in an international version of her first talking picture, *Anna Christie* (1930).

Characters whose voices one imagines: *La Glace à trois faces (The Three-Sided Mirror)* (Jean Epstein, 1927).

The police chief (I. Ivanov) in Eisenstein's *Strike* (1925).

Discussions of sound films rarely mention the voice, speaking instead of "the soundtrack." A deceptive and sloppy notion, which postulates that all the audio elements recorded together onto the optical track of the film are presented to the spectator as a sort of bloc or coalition, across from the other bloc, a no-less-fictive "image track."

And yet everyone knows from experience that nothing of the sort occurs. A film's aural elements are not received as an autonomous unit. They are immediately analyzed and distributed in the spectator's perceptual apparatus according to the relation each bears to what the spectator sees at the time. (First and foremost: according to whether you see in the image the source attributed to the sound—for example, if words are heard, whether or not you see the person who is speaking.) It's from this *instantaneous perceptual triage* that certain audio elements (essentially those referred to as synchronous, i.e., whose apparent source is visible onscreen) can be immediately "swallowed up" in the image's false depth, or relegated to the periphery of the visual field, but on alert to appear if there's a sound whose cause is temporarily put offscreen. Meanwhile, other aural elements, notably background music and offscreen commentary, are triaged to another place, an imaginary one, comparable to a proscenium.

If there is an invisible orchestra playing the film music, we might think of this proscenium as an orchestra pit like that of opera or vaudeville (it was of course a real orchestra pit during the silent era in large movie theaters). And if we hear a commentator's voice, it corresponds to a sort of podium below the screen or alongside.

These distinctly different triages of sounds emitted from the single real source of the loudspeaker, triages based on the simple criterion of each sound's relation to each image at each moment, already testify sufficiently that *there is no soundtrack*, to put it provocatively. It is the image that governs this triage, not the nature of the recorded elements themselves. The proof is that so-called synchronous sounds are most often forgotten as such, being "swallowed up" by the fiction. The meanings and effects generated by synch sounds are usually chalked up to the image alone or the film overall. Only the creators of

3

a film's sound—recordist, sound effects person, mixer, director—know that if you alter or remove these sounds, *the image is no longer the same*. On the other hand, the sounds from the proscenium, at a remove from the visual field, more easily gain the spotlight, for they are perceived in their singularity and isolation. This is why people have written much more about film music and voiceover commentary than about so-called synchronous sounds, most often neglected unjustly for being "redundant."

To see or not to see the sound's source: it all begins here, but this simple duality is already quite complex. We can suppose that there aren't just two places for the triage to go, that a sound can be non-synchronous without necessarily inhabiting the imaginary proscenium offscreen I have described. Consider as examples the "offscreen" voice of someone who has just left the image but continues to be there, or a man we've never seen but whom we expect to see, because we situate him in a place contiguous with the screen, in the present tense of the action. These sounds and voices that are *neither entirely inside nor clearly outside* are those that interest me the most, as will become amply evident. Because perhaps it is with these sounds and voices left to wander the surface of the screen that the real and specific power of the cinema comes into play.

Indeed, all the other cases or types of voices in cinema may have derived from older dramatic forms. The synchronous voice comes from the theater; film music comes from opera, melodrama, and vaudeville; and voiceover commentary from the magic lantern shows and from older arts involving narrated projections.

The cinema has its own specific devices for putting these three situations into play, but it nevertheless inherits and deploys the older genres' principles. However, sounds and voices that wander the surface of the screen, awaiting a place to attach to, belong to the cinema and to it alone. Their effect is all the more elusive in that it occurs in a context where sounds and images are ceaselessly moving and changing.

Having abruptly decreed that there is no soundtrack, let us go

4

further, and make a dent in the notion that for the filmic spectator, there are "sounds" as a collective entity—as if we received sonic messages, in films and elsewhere, in an undifferentiated and neutral way; as if our hearing weren't first and foremost human hearing.

VOCOCENTRISM   In actual movies, for real spectators, there are not *all the sounds including the human voice. There are voices, and then everything else.* In other words, in every audio mix, the presence of a human voice instantly sets up a hierarchy of perception.

Christiane Sacco elegantly writes, "The presence of a body structures the space that contains it" (meaning of course the human body).[2] Let us paraphrase this to say that *the presence of a human voice structures the sonic space that contains it.*

Near the Forum des Halles, which in 1978 was a large new shopping mall in the middle of Paris, a giant cement construction presented to the passerby the spectacle of a blind wall, an immense neutral rectangle, empty and vertical like a blank page. One day someone painted onto this surface a small walking man and his shadow—occupying about one hundredth of the wall. The moment this figure appeared, the visual space was structured entirely around him. His presence gave the space an inclination, a perspective, a left and right, a front and rear. It's the same for any sonic space, empty or not. If a human voice is part of it, the ear is inevitably carried toward it, picking it out, and structuring the perception of the whole around it. The ear attempts to analyze the sound in order to extract meaning from it—as one peels and squeezes a fruit—and always tries to *localize* and if possible *identify* the voice.

This is such a natural reflex that everything is mobilized implicitly, in the classical cinema, to favor the voice and the text it carries, and to offer it to the spectator on a silver platter. The level and presence of the voice have to be artificially enhanced over other sounds, in order to compensate for the absence of the landmarks that in live binaural conditions allow us to isolate the voice from ambient sounds. But production mixing—what in French is called "prise de son" or *taking of*

2. Christiane Sacco, *Plaidoyer au roi de Prusse ou la première anamorphose* (Paris: Buchet-Castel, 1980), p. 12.

sound during shooting—is really a "taking of voices" in most cases; the other noises are reduced as far as possible. In the same way, the technical and aesthetic norms of the classic cinema were implicitly calculated to privilege the voice and the intelligibility of dialogue. Is it not natural to ensure comprehension of what is spoken? No doubt yes, but intelligibility is not the only thing at stake. It's rather the privilege accorded to the voice over all other sonic elements, in the same way that the human face is not just an image like the others. Speech, shouts, sighs or whispers, the voice hierarchizes everything around it. Just as a mother awakes when the distant crying of her child disturbs the normal sound environment of the night, in the torrent of sounds our attention fastens first onto this other *us* that is the voice of another. Call this *vococentrism* if you will. Human listening is naturally vococentrist, and so is the talking cinema by and large.

Hitchcock said something once in an interview for *Cahiers du cinéma* that provided inspiration for my own thinking (he was speaking not of the soundtrack but of the frame): "The first thing I draw [in storyboarding], no matter what the framing, is the first thing that people will look at—faces. The position of the face determines the shot composition."[3] I had only to transpose this lucid remark to the aural register: the first thing people hear is the voice. Now I had an axis, a way to talk about *film sound* which was no longer merely a tiresome academic subject. I no longer faced the inert, heterogeneous and undifferentiated mass connoted by the catchall term "soundtrack." Just as the question of the closeup became clarified as soon as it was viewed with reference to human measure, it is by relating the question of film sound to human perception (which is naturally vococentric) that we escape the mechanistic and reductionist impasse that the notion of a soundtrack leads to. Which doesn't mean we can't refocus eventually on the other sounds, on noises and music.

WHEN THE CINEMA WAS DEAF   Jean Painlevé wrote that "the cinema has always been sound cinema." Jean Mitry specified, on the other hand, that "the early cinema was not mute, but quiet." To which Adorno

3. Interview with Alfred Hitchcock by Jean Domarchi and Jean Douchet [*Cahiers du cinéma* no. 102, 1959], reprinted in André Bazin et al., eds., *La Politique des auteurs* (Paris: Editions Champ libre, 1972), p. 153.

and Eisler replied in advance, "the talking picture, too, is mute." Indeed, corrects Bresson, "there never was a mute cinema." Besides, André Bazin noted, "But not all of silent films want to be such," and so on.[4] I throw out these few citations (out of context, to be sure) to stir the waters of pat formulas; to this I'll toss in another stone of my own in stating that the silent cinema should really be called "deaf cinema."

Prologue:
Raising the Voice

First, why do the Latin countries call silent cinema "mute cinema"? It is interesting to ask at what moment this expression arose. Logically, it would be with the birth of the talkies, when the latter retrospectively made clear that the movies that came before were *voiceless*. Not that people didn't know that; they had simply forgotten. Similarly, while we await the three-dimensional cinema of the future, we continually forget that the cinematic image is flat, although it tries to make us believe the contrary.

But the spectators and critics of 1925 didn't talk of going to see a mute film or silent film any more than we say we're going to see a talkie or sound film today. The symbolic date of 1927, the year of *The Jazz Singer*, marks the moment when the entire previous cinema was retrospectively declared silent, just as perhaps one day people will talk of the flat cinema. Today's flat cinema *dreams of depth*; and similarly the so-called mute cinema made spectators imagine the voice, far from denying or mourning its demise.

The silent film may be called deaf insofar as it prevented us from hearing the real sounds of the story. It had no ears for the immediate aural space, the here and now of the action.

But the expression "mute cinema" is what had taken hold by 1929, two years after the official birth of the talkies. In French, mute and silent are not synonymous. If the French hardly ever distinguish between sound film and talking film, they speak rarely of "silent" film. In René Clair's writings, the use of this term is an anglicism. The hesitation between mute and silent film, like the one between sound and talking film, centers on the same issue: speech, the voice.

However, could anyone rightly call this cinema silent, which was

4. Painlevé, in "Souvenirs," *Le Film français*, no. 1755 (Feb. 1979), p. 22; Mitry, *Esthétique et psychologie du cinéma*, Jean-Pierre Delarge, ed.; Hanns Eisler [and T. W. Adorno], *Composing for the Films* (New York: Oxford University Press, 1947), p.76; Bresson, interview by Michel Delahaye and Jean-Luc Godard [*Cahiers du cinéma*, no. 178, 1966], reprinted in *La Politique des auteurs*, p. 301; Bazin, *What Is Cinema?* Hugh Gray, trans. (Berkeley: University of California Press, 1971), vol. 1, p. 138.

always accompanied by music from the outset—the Lumière Brothers' very first screening at the Grand Café in Paris—not to mention the sound effects created live in some movie houses? There were also the commentators, who freely interpreted the intertitles that the audience could not read, since many moviegoers were illiterate and most were unable to cope with subtitles in foreign languages.

The movies were even less deserving of the term "mute," if by that we're supposed to understand that the characters *did not speak*. On the contrary, film characters were quite chatty. In this sense Bresson is right to say that there never was a mute cinema. "For the characters did in fact talk, only they spoke in a vacuum, no one could hear what they were saying. Thus it should not be said that the movies had found a mute style."[5] How did spectators know that the characters were speaking? By the constant movement of their lips, their gestures that told of entire speeches whose intertitles communicated to us only the most abridged versions. So it's not that the film's characters were mute, but rather that the film was deaf to them. This is the reason for using the term "deaf cinema" for films that gave the moviegoer a deaf person's viewpoint on the action depicted.

Still, this spectator who is forced to be deaf cannot avoid hearing voices—voices that resonate in his or her own imagination. As the radio listener gives a face to her favorite announcers, especially if she has never seen them (which allows her all the more freely to imagine them), likewise the silent-film spectator—rather, the deaf-film spectator—imagined the film's voices, in his or her individual way. Voices in silent film, because they are implied, are dreamed voices. Garbo in the silent era had as many voices as all of her admirers individually conferred on her. The talkie limited her to one, her own.

Had anyone ever before seen a dramatic genre for which the actor moves his lips without our hearing one word? Never, certainly not in mime, which is done with mouths closed. If for some people the talkie still seemed vulgar by comparison to the silents, it is because the real voices heard in it came into conflict with the imaginary voices that everyone could dream to their heart's content. The

5. Interview with Robert
Bresson in *La Politique des
auteurs*, p. 301.

same disappointment, the same effect of gross realism arises when on television or in a photograph we see a radio star of whose physical attributes we were previously unaware. (This revelation is becoming rare, but still occurred frequently a generation ago).

So it's not so much the *absence of voices* that the talking film came to disrupt, as the spectator's freedom to imagine them in her own way (in the same way that a filmed adaptation objectifies the features of a character in the novel). We're no longer allowed to *dream the voices*—in fact, to *dream period*: according to Marguerite Duras, the cinema has "closed off" the imaginary. "Something about the silents is lost forever. There is something vulgar, trivial . . . in the unavoidable realism of direct dialogue . . . and the inevitable trickery it involves."[6]

Which doesn't mean the cinema didn't quickly discover uses of the voice other than filming plays and musicals (uses that were by no means dishonorable). Indeed, just about all that the cinema can do structurally with the voice in a cinematic narrative can be found in one film from 1932, Fritz Lang's *Testament of Dr. Mabuse*. By "structurally" I mean here a syntax of possible relations between the film image and the voice, relationships whose types and combinations seem to be of a limited number. But just as western music has operated for several centuries on the basis of twelve notes, the cinema is far from having exhausted the possible variations on these figures. And the richest of voice-image relations, of course, isn't the arrangement that shows the person speaking, but rather the situation in which we don't see the person we hear, as his voice comes from the center of the image, the same source of all the film's other sounds. This is the cinema's invention of the *acousmêtre*.

LACKING LACK   From the moment they became heard, the voice and synch sound brought a bit of disappointment to film, the disappointment that comes from the "oral" filling of an absence or lack over which desire has built its nest. Once heard in reality, even the most divine voice had something trivial about it. But as a wise American said to Alexandre Arnoux, "Once you have given a child a doll

6. [Marguerite Duras],
Marguerite Duras (Paris:
Editions Albatros, 1975), p.
80.

that says 'papa' and 'mama,' even badly, he doesn't want any other."[7] The dazzling success of the sound film, which to everyone's surprise profoundly shook up the film industry, demonstrated the strong allure of talkies. Perhaps what people sought there was the same kind of oral satisfaction that today's special visual effects and Dolby stereo give us, this hyper-nurturing cinema whose sensory realism may offend the cinephile's sensibility but that brings on a sort of beatitude. In the same way, the talking films (leaving aside the transitional part-talkies) were not good at tolerating lack, i.e. silence, even though they authorized silence as a new creative element.

The early sound film *lacked lack*, so to speak; some time had to pass before the magical and cloying effect of hyperrealism would abate, and for the reappearance of the lack necessary for the sound film's full functioning.

It should not be assumed that the cinema began to talk in a single moment. In 1895 Thomas Edison first tried to invent sound film. Which was possible technically; the gramophone as well as the telephone were already well in place before cinema. The idea of reproducing reality by coupling sound and image in synch motivated many of film's pioneer inventors. Between 1895 and 1927, between the *Workers Leaving the Lumière Factory* and *The Jazz Singer*, sound film patents number in the dozens, as do the public demonstrations of talking pictures in commercial cinemas (such as the Gaumont-Palace in Paris).

By 1905, processes such as Phono-Ciné-Théâtre, Tonbild, and the Bio-Phonographe could present to audiences a scene from *Hamlet* with Sarah Bernhardt, *with voices*, or a filmed opera like Gounod's *Faust*, *with sound*. The means of synchronization weren't reliable, though, especially for longer stretches, and the cinema—aesthetically as well as commercially—pursued other directions. This is why, until the watershed of 1927, these numerous experiments remained little more than curiosities.

Reading the newspapers of the time announce these demonstrations of talking cinema before its official birth, we're struck not by the writers' lyrical transports but rather the calmness with which

7. René Clair, *Cinema Yesterday and Today*, R. C. Dale, ed., Stanley Appelbaum, trans. (New York: Dover, 1972 [1970]), p. 148.

they describe it. The public was doubtless acquainted with the idea
of talking films if not their reality. They were invited to see them as
we are today to see holograms—prepared for, yet amazed by, a new
technology still applied only to modest ends. Although all histories
of cinema allude to this plethora of sound experiments to one extent
or another, they still don't challenge the neat division (statistically
based) of film history into a silent period and a sound period.

The so-called silent cinema was thus a sort of lame duck for a long
while, quite aware of a change in store. What remained unknown at
the time was what would become of the sound film in the long run.
But in 1929, or two years after its "birth," many had already made up
their minds. Sound film, they claimed, was only good for filmed theater or musical comedy; ascribing artistic dignity to it was out of the
question. For others, the cinema could only hope to acquire such dignity through such phenomena as *audiovisual counterpoint*. Pudovkin,
Eisenstein, and Alexandrov's manifesto argued against using sounds
as flat literal illustrations of images, and in favor of audiovisual counterpoint, wherein sounds declare their independence and act
metaphorically, symbolically. And who at the time could foresee the
role to be played by the new entity we call the acousmêtre?

If moviegoers were enthusiastic about the talking film—and such
was the case for the vast majority—they could enjoy being carried
away by its sensory rush. But if people wanted to look for its short-
comings (as we do today for films in stereo), they could note with
Alexandre Arnoux the effect of voices being "glued" onto bodies, and
the perceptible mismatch between the position of characters' mouths
onscreen and the real source of the sound (the central loudspeaker behind the screen). Today our brains are entirely accustomed to plugging
sounds into whatever images we see—sounds whose real localization
is much more dispersed and dissociated with respect to what we see.

THE VOICE'S LOSS OF INNOCENCE In a period when the new talking film was
contested by such major artists as Chaplin, Eisenstein, and Stroheim,
we might well ask why there was so little discussion of the voice in

itself, since it was the voice that truly constituted the great revolution.

It *was* discussed, of course. It's just that instead of saying "the voice," people said "speech" or "dialogue," putting the focus on language. But since there was already language and speech in the silent film, it was the *voice* and not language that was the problem. Greta Garbo's voice was hoarse and had a Swedish accent: the producers of her first talkie, *Anna Christie*, wondered whether audiences would put up with it. John Gilbert's somewhat high and nasal voice spelled the ruin of his career. The voices of American actors brought British audiences to laughter . . . It's against the voice that Chaplin was really protesting, under the name of speech. Sound, on the other hand, didn't bother him, since he made *sonorized* films until 1935.

As film began to talk, the problem was not text; silent cinema had already integrated text through the bastard device of intertitles. It was the voice, as material presence, as utterance, or as muteness—the voice as being, double, shadow of the image, as a power—the voice as a threat of loss and seduction for the cinema.

"To use sound [as naturalistic speech]," said the three Russians' manifesto, "will destroy the culture of montage." René Clair contemplated the talkie as a "frightful monster," and French film historians Bardèche and Brasillach issued this suggestion: "We who have witnessed the birth of an art may also have witnessed its death." In a word, the fantasy of *the death of cinema* was alive and well, as it is today at the beginning of the 1980s. The reasons are no doubt different. It is perhaps only a coincidence that the voice figures prominently today as a theoretical object simultaneously with the appearance of films like Marguerite Duras's *L'Homme Atlantique*, in which a woman's voice announces, during a marvelous speech about love, the end of cinema. All this may be only a French phenomenon, coinciding accidentally with revolutionary technological developments (high definition video, new audio processes, home video distribution of films) that mark the end of cinema as we know it.

That the voice has today become a subject of discussion and theoretical study does not mean, of course, that people are going to make more interesting uses of it in the future. The cinema could be losing the authenticity that allowed movies until now to engage the voice in such immediate and striking ways. Films like *The Testament of Dr. Mabuse*, *Psycho*, *Sansho the Bailiff*, and *India Song*, in which the powers of the voice are brought into play with singular imaginative force, belong perhaps to an age forever past—the voice's Age of Innocence.

It was necessary to lose this innocence before we could perceive it as such. Perhaps there is so much writing on the voice now because there has been a break, a separation from that innocence. But this break testifies to a change in our sensibility, and of investment in a new cinematic object: the voice, from the same unchangeable mythology of paradise lost.

I. MABUSE: THE MAGIC AND POWER OF THE ACOUSMÊTRE

Elsie (Inge Landgut) meets
the murderer's shadow in *M*
(Fritz Lang, 1931).

ONE THE ACOUSMÊTRE

A PRIMAL HIDE-AND-SEEK Human vision, like that of cinema, is partial and directional. Hearing, though, is omnidirectional. We cannot see what is behind us, but we can hear all around. Of all the senses hearing is probably the earliest to occur. The fetus takes in the mother's voice, and will recognize it after birth. Sight comes into play only after birth, but at least in our culture, it becomes the most highly structured sense. It takes on a remarkable variety of forms and disposes of a highly elaborated language, which dwarfs the vocabularies for phenomena of touch, smell, and even hearing. Sight is generally what we rely on for orientation, because the naming and recognition of forms is vastly more subtle and precise in visual terms than with any other channel of perception.

The sense of hearing is as subtle as it is archaic. We most often relegate it to the limbo of the unnamed; something you hear causes you to feel X, but you can't put exact words to it. As surprising as it may seem, it wasn't until the twentieth century that Pierre Schaeffer first attempted to develop a language for describing sounds *in themselves*.[1]

In the infant's experience, the mother ceaselessly plays hide-and-seek with his visual field, whether she goes behind him, or is hidden from him by something, or if he's right up against her body and cannot see her. But the olfactory and vocal continuum, and frequently tactile contact as well, maintain the mother's presence when she can no longer be seen (in fact, *seeing* her implies at least some distance and separation). This dialectic of appearance and disappearance is known to be dramatic for the child. The cinema transposes or crystallizes it into certain ways of mobilizing offscreen space (e.g., masking characters but keeping their presence perceivable through sound). In some ways, film editing has to do with the appearance-disappearance of the mother, and also with games like the "Fort-Da" game to which Freud refers and which Lacan analyzes as a model of

1. See Schaeffer, *Traité des objets musicaux* (Paris: Le Seuil, 1966).

the "repetitive utterances in which subjectivity brings together mastery over its abandonment and the birth of the symbol."[2]

Onscreen and offscreen space can thus be called by another name when what's involved is the voice "maintaining" a character who has left the screen, or better yet, when the film obstinately refuses to show us someone whose voice we hear: it's a game of hide-and-seek.

NEITHER INSIDE NOR OUTSIDE   We know that the invention of talking pictures allowed people to hear the actors' voices, for example to put a voice to the face of Garbo. Perhaps more interesting is that the sound film can show a closed door or an opaque curtain and allow us to hear the voice of someone supposedly behind it. Sound films can show an empty space and give us the voice of someone supposedly "there," in the scene's "here and now," but outside the frame. A voice may inhabit the emptiest image, or even the dark screen, as Ophuls makes it do in *Le Plaisir*, Welles in *The Magnificent Ambersons*, and Duras in *L'Homme Atlantique*, with an *acousmatic presence*.

Acousmatic, specifies an old dictionary, "is said of a sound that is heard without its cause or source being seen." We can never praise Pierre Schaeffer enough for having unearthed this arcane word in the 1950s. He adopted it to designate a mode of listening that is commonplace today, systematized in the use of radio, telephones, and phonograph records. Of course, it existed long before any of these media, but for lack of a specific label, wasn't obviously identifiable, and surely was rarely conceived as such in experience. On the other hand, Schaeffer did not see fit for his purposes (he was interested in *musique concrète*) to find a specific word for the flip side of acousmatic listening, the apparently trivial situation wherein we do see the sound source. He was content to speak in this case of "direct" listening. Since his term is ambiguous, we prefer to speak of *visualized listening*.[3]

The talking film naturally began with *visualized* sound (often called synchronous or onscreen sound). But it quickly turned to experimenting with acousmatic sound—not only music but more importantly the voice. Critics often cite an early scene in Fritz Lang's *M*

2. Jacques Lacan, *Écrits* (Paris: Editions du Seuil, 1966), p. 318; Anthony Wilden, trans., *Speech and Language in Psychoanalysis* (Lacan's 1953 "Discours de Rome") (Baltimore: Johns Hopkins University Press, 1981 [1968]), p. 318.

3. Since the terms most often used, *offscreen* and *nondiegetic*, are much too ambiguous, I use acousmatic to replace them.

[Schaeffer and Chion's "acousmatic" does not appear in English-language dictionaries. The word's source is the Greek "akousma," a thing heard. See also note 5. *Trans.*]

(1930) as an example. The child-murderer's shadow falls on the poster that offers a reward for his capture, while his offscreen voice says to the little girl (she is also offscreen at this moment, contrary to the evidence of the famous production still): "You have a pretty ball!" The copresence in this shot of the voice and the shadow, as well as the use of the acousmatic voice to create tension, are eloquent enough. But fairly quickly in the development of sound film, the voice would stand alone without "needing" either the shadow or other narrative devices, such as superimposition, to present acousmatic characters.

We should emphasize that between one (visualized) situation and the other (acousmatic) one, it's not the sound that changes its nature, presence, distance, or color. What changes is the relationship between what we see and what we hear. The murderer's voice is just as well-defined when we don't see him as in any shot where we do. When we listen to a film without watching it, it is impossible to distinguish acousmatic from visualized sounds solely on the basis of the soundtrack. Just listening, without the images, "acousmatizes" all the sounds, if they retain no trace of their initial relation to the image. (And in this case, the aggregate of sounds heard becomes a true "sound track," a whole).[4]

To understand what is at stake in this distinction, let us go back to the original meaning of the word acousmatic. This was apparently the name assigned to a Pythagorean sect whose followers would listen to their Master speak *behind a curtain*, as the story goes, so that the sight of the speaker wouldn't distract them from the message.[5] (In the same way, television makes it easy to be distracted from what a person on-screen is talking about; we might watch the way she furrows her eyebrows or fidgets with her hands; cameras lovingly emphasize such details.) This interdiction against looking, which transforms the Master, God, or Spirit into an acousmatic voice, permeates a great number of religious traditions, most notably Islam and Judaism. We find it also in the physical setup of Freudian analysis: the patient on the couch should not see the analyst, who does not look at him. And finally we find it in the cinema, where the voice of the acousmatic master who hides behind a door, a curtain or offscreen, is at play in some key films:

4. Cf. Prologue, "There Is No Soundtrack."

5. The history of the term is interesting. The French word *acousmate* designates "invisible" sounds. Apollinaire, who loved rare words, wrote a poem in 1913 entitled "Acousmate," about a voice that resonates in the air. The famous *Encyclopédie* of Diderot and d'Alembert (1751) cites the "Acousmatiques" as those uninitiated disciples of Pythagoras who were obliged to spend five years in silence listening to their master speak behind the curtain, at the end of which they could look at him and were full members of the sect. It seems that Clement of Alexandria, an ecclesiastic writing around 250 BC, may be the sole source of this story, in his book *Stromateis*.

The writer Jérôme Peignot called this term to the attention of Pierre Schaeffer.

19

TOP: Didier Flamand, Delphine Seyrig, and Claude
Mann in *India Song* (Marguerite Duras, 1974).
BOTTOM: Gary Lockwood and Keir Dullea in *2001: A
Space Odyssey* (Stanley Kubrick, 1968).

The Testament of Dr. Mabuse (the voice of the evil genius), *Psycho* (the mother's voice), *The Magnificent Ambersons* (the director's voice).

When the acousmatic presence is a voice, and especially when this voice has not yet been visualized—that is, when we cannot yet connect it to a face—we get a special being, a kind of talking and acting shadow to which we attach the name *acousmêtre*.[6] A person you talk to on the phone, whom you've never seen, is an acousmêtre. If you have ever seen her, however, or if in a film you continue to hear her after she leaves the visual field, is this still an acousmêtre? Definitely, but of another kind, which we'll call the already visualized acousmêtre. It would be amusing to invent more and more neologisms, for example to distinguish whether or not we can put a face to the invisible voice.

However, I prefer to leave the definition of the acousmêtre open, to keep it generic on purpose, thus avoiding the tendency to subdivide *ad infinitum*. Let's say I am going to concentrate primarily on what may be called the *complete acousmêtre*, the one who is not-yet-seen, but who remains liable to appear in the visual field at any moment. The already visualized acousmêtre, the one temporarily absent from the picture, is more familiar and reassuring—even though in the dark regions of the acousmatic field, which surrounds the visible field, this kind can acquire by contagion some of the powers of the complete acousmêtre. Also more familiar is the commentator-acousmêtre, he who never shows himself but who has no personal stake in the image. Which powers and which stakes come into play, we shall examine further on.

But what of the acousmêtres of the radio, and the backstage voice in the theater and the opera? Are these not of the same cloth, and are we perhaps just pompously reinventing the radio announcer or the actor-in-the-wings?

The radio-acousmêtre. It should be evident that the radio is acousmatic by nature. People speaking on the radio are acousmêtres in that there's no possibility of seeing them; this is the essential difference between them and the filmic acousmêtre. In radio one cannot play with showing, partially showing, and not showing.

6. The French term is a neologism made from "être acousmatique," or acousmatic being.

In film, the acousmatic zone is defined as fluctuating, constantly subject to challenge by what we might see. Even in an extreme case like Marguerite Duras's film *Son nom de Venise dans Calcutta désert*, in whose deserted images we hardly ever see the faces and bodies that belong to the acousmêtres who populate the soundtrack (the same soundtrack as *India Song*'s), the principle of cinema is that at any moment these faces and bodies *might* appear, and thereby de-acousmatize the voices. Another thing: in the cinema, unlike on the radio, what we have seen and heard makes us prejudge what we don't see, and the possibility of deception always lurks as well. Cinema has a frame, whose edges are visible; we can see where the frame leaves off and offscreen space starts. In radio, we cannot perceive where things "cut," as sound itself has no frame.

The theater-acousmêtre. Georges Sadoul, in his *History of Cinema*, yields to the temptation to associate experiments in "audio-visual counterpoint" in the early sound era with "traditional offstage sounds in the theater."[7] But between an offstage voice and a filmic acousmêtre there is more than a shade of difference.

In the theater, the offstage voice is clearly heard coming from another space than the stage—it's literally located elsewhere. The cinema does not employ a *stage*, even if from time to time it might simulate one, but rather a *frame*, with variable points of view. In this frame, visualized voices and acousmatic voices are recognized as such only in the spectator's head, depending on what she sees. In most cases, offscreen sound comes from the same actual place as the other sounds—a central loudspeaker.[8] There are of course ambiguous cases when we can't easily distinguish what is "offscreen" from what is in the visual field (Fellini's films are rich in examples). But it should go without saying that the presence of such ambiguity does not make the distinction between offscreen and onscreen any less pertinent.

So we are a long way from the theatrical offstage voice, which we concretely perceive at a remove from the stage. Unlike the film frame the theater's stage doesn't make you jump from one angle of vision

7. Sadoul, *Histoire du cinéma mondial* (Paris: Flammarion, 1963), p. 234.

8. [Recall that these remarks were written in 1981, at a time when many French movie theaters were not outfitted for multitrack sound. Dolby and multitrack change the rules of the game—but not as much as one might think. Often, sound editors avoid locating an offscreen diegetic sound on a prolonged basis because the logic of cutting threatens to disrupt the logic of screen space. *Trans.*]

22

to another, from closeup to long shot. For the spectator, then, the filmic acousmêtre is "offscreen," outside the image, and at the same time *in* the image: the loudspeaker that's actually its source is located behind the image in the movie theater.[9] It's as if the voice were wandering along the surface, *at once inside and outside*, seeking a place to settle. Especially when a film hasn't yet shown what body this voice normally inhabits.

Neither inside nor outside: such is the acousmêtre's fate in the cinema.

WHAT ARE THE ACOUSMÊTRE'S POWERS?   Everything hangs on whether or not the acousmêtre has been seen. In the case where it remains not-yet-seen, even an insignificant acousmatic voice becomes invested with magical powers as soon as it is involved, however slightly, in the image. The powers are usually malevolent, occasionally tutelary. Being involved in the image means that the voice doesn't merely speak as an observer (as commentary), but that it bears with the image a relationship of *possible inclusion*, a relationship of power and possession capable of functioning in both directions; the image may contain the voice, or the voice may contain the image.

The not-yet-seen voice (e.g. Mabuse's in *The Testament*, or Maupassant's in the first two parts of Ophuls' *Le Plaisir*) possesses a sort of virginity, derived from the simple fact that the body that's supposed to emit it has not yet been inscribed in the visual field. Its *de-acousmatization*, which results from finally showing the person speaking, is always like a deflowering. For at that point the voice loses its virginal-acousmatic powers, and re-enters the realm of human beings.

The counterpart to the not-yet-seen voice is the body that has not yet spoken—the silent character (not to be confused with the character in the silent movie). These two characters, the acousmêtre and the mute, are similar in some striking ways[10].

An entire image, an entire story, an entire film can thus hang on the epiphany of the acousmêtre. Everything can boil down to a quest

9. Furthermore, we imagine it there in TV, at the drive-in, and so on.

10. See Chapter 7 on silent and mute characters in film.

to bring the acousmêtre into the light. In this description we can recognize *Mabuse* and *Psycho*, but also numerous mystery, gangster, and
fantasy films that are all about "defusing" the acousmêtre, who is the
hidden monster, or the Big Boss, or the evil genius, or on rare occasions a wise man. The acousmêtre, as we have noted, cannot occupy
the removed position of commentator, the voice of the magic
lantern show. He must, even if only slightly, have *one foot in the image*,
in the space of the film; he must haunt the borderlands that are neither the interior of the filmic stage nor the proscenium—a place that
has no name, but which the cinema forever brings into play.

Being in the screen and not, wandering the surface of the screen
without entering it, the acousmêtre brings disequilibrium and tension.
He invites the spectator to *go see*, and he can be an *invitation to the loss
of the self, to desire and fascination.* But what is there to fear from the
acousmêtre? And what are his powers?

The powers are four: the ability to be everywhere, to see all, to
know all, and to have complete power. In other words: ubiquity,
panopticism, omniscience, and omnipotence.

The acousmêtre is everywhere, its voice comes from an immaterial
and non-localized body, and it seems that no obstacle can stop it.
Media such as the telephone and radio, which send acousmatic voices traveling and which enable them to be here and there at once,
often serve as vehicles of this ubiquity. In *2001,* Hal, the talking computer, inhabits the entire space ship.

The acousmêtre is all-seeing, its word is like the word of God: "No
creature can hide from it." The one who is not in the visual field is in
the best position to see everything that's happening. The one you
don't see is in the best position to see you—at least this is the power
you attribute to him. You might turn around to try to surprise him,
since he could always be behind you. This is the paranoid and often
obsessional *panoptic fantasy,* which is the fantasy of total mastery of
space by vision.

A good number of films are based on the idea of the all-seeing
voice. In Fritz Lang's *Testament of Dr. Mabuse* the master's look pierces

through an opaque curtain. In *2001* the computer Hal, a voice-being, uncannily starts reading the astronauts' lips even when they have incapacitated its hearing. Many films classically feature a narrator's voice which, from its removed position, can see everything. And there are the voices of invisible ghosts who move about wherever the action goes, and from whom nothing can be hidden (Ophuls' *Tendre Ennemie*). And of course thrillers often feature telephone voices that terrorize their victims to the tune of "you can't see me, but I see you."[11]

A John Carpenter horror film, *The Fog*, enacts the panoptic fantasy in a particularly ingenious form. The film's heroine, played by Adrienne Barbeau, works as a disc jockey at a local radio station perched atop an old lighthouse, from where she can see the entire city. The film's other characters know her only as a voice that is uniquely in the position to see the predicament they are in (the town invaded by an evil cloud). The fog makes them lose their bearings and the only thing that cuts through it is the voice of the airwaves, which broadcasts from the lighthouse, materializing its panoptic power.

The all-seeing acousmêtre appears to be the rule. The exception, or anomaly, is the voice of the acousmêtre who does not see all; here we find the panoptic theme in its negative form. In Josef von Sternberg's *Saga of Anatahan*, the action takes place on an island where Japanese soldiers have been marooned; we hear them speaking in Japanese. For the Western spectator, these scenes, instead of being dubbed or subtitled, have an English-language voiceover commentary spoken by Sternberg himself. He speaks in the name of the band of soldiers, employing a strange "we." This "we" refers not to the entire group, but to most of them—the ones excluded from contact with the only woman on the island. In fact, when the image and synch dialogue in Japanese bring us into the shack to discover the woman with her partner of the moment, the narrator speaks with the voice of someone who cannot see what is before our eyes, and who only imagines it ("We were not able to find out"). Contrary to the camera's eye, the narrator has not gone inside the shack. The dissociation between the acousmetric narrator's voice and the camera's

The Acousmêtre

11. [See the Epilogue on recent uses of the telephone in horror films. *Trans.*]

25

indiscreet gaze is all the more disconcerting in that the voice claiming not to be looking is in the very place from which film voices can normally see everything—i.e., offscreen—and it's hard to believe that the voice is not privy to the action onscreen. We'd prefer to suppose that it's a bit dishonest about its partial blindness. The "we" in whose name it speaks seems not to refer to anyone in particular; you cannot detect which specific individual among the soldiers has taken charge of the storytelling.

In much the same way, acousmatic voices heard as we see Marguerite Duras's *India Song* speak as unseeing voices. This not-seeing-all, not-knowing-all occurs first in connection with the couple consisting of the Vice-Consul and Anne-Marie Stretter, just like that of Sternberg's "we" applies to the couple in the hut. This and other examples we will examine suggest that the *partially-seeing acousmêtre* has something to do with the primal scene. *What it claims not to see* is what the couple is doing. Bertolucci's film *Tragedy of a Ridiculous Man* revolves around a perverse inversion of the primal scene. It is the father who does not see what the son is doing with . . . as I take it, the mother. The father has received as a present from the son a pair of binoculars with which, on the roof of his factory, he enjoys the power of looking at everything going on. Bertolucci has endowed the father (Ugo Tognazzi) with a singular "internal voice." We cannot tell where the father's voice's vision and knowledge end, especially with regard to the son whom "it" sees being kidnapped, and with regard to everything that happens behind his back of which "it" sees nothing.

The most disconcerting, in fact, is not when we attribute unlimited knowledge to the acousmêtre, but rather when its vision and knowledge have limits whose dimensions we do not know. The idea of a god who sees and knows all (the gods of Judaism, Christianity, and Islam are acousmêtres) is perhaps an "indecent" idea, according to the little girl Nietzsche writes of, but it is almost natural. Much more disturbing is the idea of a god or being with only partial powers and vision, whose limits are not known.

26

The acousmêtre's omniscience and omnipotence. By discussing the acousmêtre's supposed capacity to see all, we have set the stage for considering the powers that follow from this. Seeing all, in the logic of magical thought we are exploring, implies knowing all; knowledge has been assimilated into the capacity to see internally. Also implied is omnipotence, or at the least the possession of certain powers whose nature or extent can vary—invulnerability, control over destructive forces, hypnotic power, and so on.

Why all these powers in a voice? Maybe because this *voice without a place* that belongs to the acousmêtre takes us back to an archaic, original stage: of the first months of life or even before birth, during which the voice was everything and it was everywhere (but bear in mind that this "everywhere" quality is nameable only retrospectively—the concept can arise for the subject who no longer occupies the undifferentiated everywhere).

The sound film is therefore not just a stage inhabited by speaking simulacra, as in Bioy Casares' novella *The Invention of Morel*. The sound film also has an offscreen field that can be populated by acousmatic voices, founding voices, determining voices—voices that command, invade, and vampirize the image; voices that often have the omnipotence to guide the action, call it up, make it happen, and sometimes lose it on the borderline between land and sea. Of course, the sound film did not invent the acousmêtre. The greatest Acousmêtre is God—and even farther back, for every one of us, the Mother. But the sound film invented for the acousmêtre a space of action that no dramatic form had succeeded in giving to it; this happened once the coming of sound placed the cinema *at the mercy of the voice*.

DE-ACOUSMATIZATION Such are the powers of the acousmêtre. Of course, the acousmêtre has only to show itself—for the person speaking to inscribe his or her body inside the frame, in the visual field— for it to lose its power, omniscience, and (obviously) ubiquity. I call this phenomenon de-acousmatization. *Embodying the voice* is a sort of symbolic act, dooming the acousmêtre to the fate of ordinary mortals. De-acousmatization roots the acousmêtre to a place and says, "here is your body, you'll be there, and not elsewhere." Likewise, the purpose of burial ceremonies is to say to the soul of the deceased, "you must no longer wander, your grave is here."

In how many fantasy, thriller, and gangster films do we see the acousmêtre become an ordinary person when his voice is assigned a visible and circumscribed body? He then usually becomes, if not harmless, at least human and vulnerable. When the heretofore invisible Big Boss appears in the image, we generally know that he's going to be captured or brought down "like just any imbecile" (as Pascal Bonitzer says in talking about Aldrich's *Kiss Me Deadly*).[12]

De-acousmatization, the unveiling of an image and at the same time a *place*, the human and mortal body where the voice will henceforth be lodged, in certain ways strongly resembles striptease. The process doesn't necessarily happen all at once; it can be progressive. In much the same way that the female genitals are the end point revealed by undressing (the point after which the denial of the absence of the penis is no longer possible), there is an end point of de-acousmatization—the *mouth* from which the voice issues. So we can have semi-acousmêtres, or on the other hand partial de-acousmatizations, when we haven't yet seen the mouth of a character who speaks, and we just see his hand, back, feet, or neck. A quarter-acousmêtre is even possible—its head facing the camera, but the mouth hidden! As long as the face and mouth have not been completely revealed, and as long as the spectator's eye has not "verified" the co-incidence of the voice with the mouth (a verification which needs only to be approximate), de-acousmatization is incomplete, and the voice retains an aura of invulnerability and magical power.

The Wizard of Oz (1939) has a lovely scene of de-acousmatization that illustrates these points well. "The Great Oz" is the name that author L. Frank Baum gave his magician character. He speaks with a booming voice in a sort of temple, hiding behind an apparatus of curtains, grimacing masks, and smoke. This thundering voice

12. Pascal Bonitzer, *Le Regard et la voix* (Paris: Union Générale d'Editions, 1976), p. 32.

28

seemingly sees all and knows all; it can tell Dorothy and her friends what they have come for even before they've opened their mouths. But when they return to get their due once they've accomplished their mission, the wizard refuses to keep his promise and starts playing for time. Dorothy is indignant; her dog Toto wanders toward the voice, tears the curtain behind which the voice is hidden, and reveals an ordinary little fellow who's speaking into a microphone and operating reverb and smoke machines. The Great Oz is nothing but a man, who enjoys playing God by hiding his body and amplifying his voice. And the moment this voice is "embodied," we can hear it lose its colossal proportions, deflate and become a wisp of a voice, finally speaking as a human. "You are a naughty man," says Dorothy. "Oh no, my dear," timidly replies the former magician, "I am a very nice man, but a very bad magician." For Dorothy this de-acousmatization marks the end of her initiation, this moment when she mourns the loss of parental omnipotence and uncovers the mortal and fallible Father.

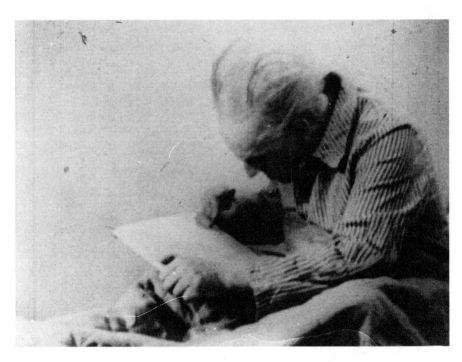

Rudolf Klein-Rogge in *The
Testament of Dr. Mabuse*
(Fritz Lang, 1932).

In 1931 when Fritz Lang and Thea von Harbou came up with a sequel to their 1922 silent film *Dr. Mabuse the Gambler*, and reenlisted their psychopathic evil genius Mabuse to engage in new adventures, expectations ran high. Since the cinema had just gained a new weapon, the voice, nothing would be easier than to endow the diabolical hypnotist with a resounding voice and announce to the audience, "Mabuse speaks," just as the publicity campaign for *Anna Christie* used the slogan "Garbo speaks!"

Instead, they did the opposite, a superb idea even if the child of circumstance. They would use the talking film precisely *not* to let viewers hear the voice of Mabuse. Or rather, their new film wouldn't attach his voice explicitly to a human body. The voice attributed to Mabuse—which turns out to be the voice of another—is heard only from behind a curtain. As for the veritable, authentic, original Mabuse, the Mabuse to whom Rudolf Klein-Rogge lent forever his aquiline features, he remains obstinately silent until his death. Never is he seen speaking except as a ghost or in superimposition, endowed with the eerie voice of an old witch. And it is because the living Mabuse is silent that the voice speaking in his name from behind the curtain, rooted in no body, can exercise the diabolical powers attributed to him. The terrible Mabuse is divided up into a mute body and a bodiless voice, only to rule all the more powerfully.

It can always be argued that the authors of *The Testament of Dr. Mabuse*—since this was the title of Mabuse's new adventures—had good reason to make Mabuse a silent character: Rudolf Klein-Rogge didn't speak French. *The Testament* was indeed shot in two languages, in German and French, as was the practice at the time, using the same sets but different actors. The studios had worked out this costly means to produce films for foreign distribution, as dubbing was not yet entirely feasible. But apparently Lang and von Harbou insisted on having their star play in the French version as well as the German. It was a trick to imagine that Mabuse, who was nothing if not chatty in his first adventures in silent cinema (though of course we didn't hear his voice), had fallen into some kind of mutism at the start of his talkie exploits. The voice speaking in his name was detached from his body, and would be embodied only by different actors. There you have the common sense explanation of Mabuse's silence. The idea is clever; Lang's brilliance resided in drawing from this idea the wildest possible consequences in the scenario itself.

1. At first glance, the narrative structure of *The Testament* resembles a necklace made out of short scenes strung together like pearls. In the beginning they seem to have no clear connection, but little by little they start to "clasp," to resonate with logic. At the beginning we have on one hand the silent Mabuse, and on the other there's a voice speaking in his name and surviving his death—which occurs about one-third of the way through. The plot resolution provides the rational answers to all the mysteries; the voice without a body we heard behind the curtain turns out to be the voice of Dr. Baum, the asylum director, whom Mabuse had hypnotized to submit to his will. To all appearances, the "right voice" is restored to the right body, and the speaking body, the *anacousmètre*, is reassembled. Curtain.

A first screening of the film leaves us fairly well satisfied; the story resolution seems to answer every question. Yet the more you watch it, the more you notice that the circle never quite closes. Never do we see Baum when he's speaking as Mabuse, but we *deduce* that it is he speaking, simply because that's how Kent identifies the voice he hears through Baum's office door. In other words, Kent only recognizes in a mediated voice (on a phonograph record) another mediated voice (on a loudspeaker). Not only do we never see Baum speak, we do not know where he is; we know only that he's someplace other than we thought.

How can it be that the spectator, allowed to see and hear more than any characters in the film, isn't certain she can recognize Baum's voice in its three manifestations—in the flesh, behind the curtain, and through the office door? Because identifying a voice is an elusive and difficult proposition. In a film, a voice has to have strongly marked personal characteristics, such as an accent or other distinct quality like hoarseness, to be identified with certainty. This is why the voice is often used to deceive, and why it's easy to make one voice speak as if it belongs to someone else.

2. What do we see behind the curtain that Kent tears down in his attempt to unmask the acousmêtre? Instead of the man we would expect to see face to face, we discover a technical apparatus: a microphone, a speaker horn, and the cutout silhouette which, backlit against the curtain, served falsely to indicate the presence of the Chief. But if this setup is supposed to explain everything, isn't there still something missing? Yes—the eye of the camera.

The voice has been behaving as a *voice that sees*, reacting in real time to the slightest gesture of those who are summoned before the curtain. Where is the optic machinery, the proxy for the eye, since we're being shown proxies for the voice and ear? Nowhere. The voice's power to see is somehow left to magic, to what the characters refer to as "Fernhypnose" (tele-hypnosis, or hypnosis at a distance). Of course, television hadn't yet been invented, but the idea already existed. A prefiguration of television appears in *Metropolis* (1926), but it's in the form of a *screen*, while the action of *Mabuse* would logically call for a *camera*. Showing the screen and showing the camera are two different problems. In the latter case, it's both an eye and a machine that have to be shown, and one would have to figure out how to put this into concretely visual form. Lang's final Mabuse film (*The Thousand Eyes of Dr. Mabuse*, 1961) does in fact end by "showing the camera," in the simplified form of numerous eyes set into the moldings of the ceiling.

I am struck by the fact that no one seems bothered by this absence of a camera—neither Kent and Lily, who never mention it (just as they say not a word about the technical apparatus they discover, never bringing it up with each other or with Lohmann), nor the spectator. It is possible that the unshowable camera appears before the stunned Kent and Lily looking toward us (with a look that is almost a "camera-look," as it is appropriately called in French). But the reverse shot that shows us what they see does not show it; this camera would be the very camera used in shooting the film—unfilmable by definition because it cannot film its reflection in a mirror.

The film leads us to think that there is no need for a visual organ to see through walls and across distances, because *the eye is in the very voice of the acousmêtre*.

3. And what do we finally discover, in Baum's office, after having broken through the private door behind which the same "I am not to be disturbed now" has been heard each time someone moved the door handle to enter? A second setup of mechanical equipment, an ingenious system that starts the record onto which "I'm not to be disturbed now" has been recorded. It's the intruder himself who, by moving the handle, activates the voice that forbids his entry. We learn from this that the only obstacle to restoring the acousmatic voice to its source is our own voluntary blindness, the desire to believe in the Chief's power. As in *Oz*, all is revealed to be stage machinery, *trompe-l'oreille*, capable of tricking precisely those who wish to be taken in.

The unveiling of the machine, however, conceals the most important thing from us, the elephant in the room so to speak, which again neither the spectator nor the characters seem concerned about. During that time, where are those who are absent, neither behind the door nor behind the curtain, and what are they doing?

We never see the quarters from which Mabuse-Baum gives his orders when his henchmen appear before the curtain. In one such scene, in fact, the editing gives the impression that Baum is *simultane-*

ously in his office reading, and the source of the voice behind the curtain. (The American print, re-edited and dubbed under Lang's supervision, drastically changes the editing precisely to erase these flaws in narrative logic, but here I am speaking of the original German version).

Two scenes, then, involve a de-acousmatization process, revealing unexpected things behind the curtain and the door. In both, instead of the Chief we find an assemblage of equipment for vocal projection. The scenes actually function to *conceal*, in two senses. First, they put off until another time and place—i.e., to forever and nowhere—the true unveiling of the acousmêtre. Second, and above all, they conceal from us the fact that this elsewhere does not exist.

The result is that when the film ends, apparently giving closure to the story—having identified Baum with the dead Mabuse whose place he takes (just as by the end of *Psycho* Norman in the holding cell is totally inhabited by his dead mother)—all the disparate elements are still mixed-up pieces of a puzzle; the plot pretends they fit together but they don't. This ever mute body of a Dr. Mabuse who soon becomes a corpse, once his Testament is all written; this Testament that he composes in automatic writing, and to which he gives birth in a quasi-monstrous fashion; this bug-eyed ghost of Mabuse who appears twice to Baum, with the stylized features of the Doctor but the androgynous squeaky whisper of a possessed sorcerer; this other voice, virile and firm, of the acousmêtre that speaks in Mabuse's name from behind a curtain; this Baum who's not there when he is supposed to be in his office, but who *is* there when logically he should be someplace else; and finally this name of Mabuse that circulates in various written and spoken forms—all these elements are never presented in a way that would allow us to reconstitute an integrated body, voice, and name, an *anacousmêtre* that could henceforth be circumscribed, understood, mastered, and that would be a mortal and vulnerable man.

The intellectual game with the spectator extends so far as to cause doubt that the Chief behind the curtain is Mabuse as he claims to be. And when Kent recognizes behind the office door the same voice he had heard behind the curtain, he exclaims, "That's the Chief's voice!" without uttering the name that would bring together all these disconnected elements. Between the name uttered and the name written, the silent body of the Doctor and the speaking body of Baum, the voice of Baum split into the voice of the anacousmêtre and the voice of the Chief—Lang's film starts to feel like one of those sliding-tile puzzles. Hardly do you move one square, sure of putting the picture in the right order, than you find a hole somewhere else. It might be said that having gone to all the trouble of concocting a Mabuse that was such an elusive acousmêtre that the character was literally non-de-acousmatizable, the creators of the *Testament* took pleasure in doing *everything* in one film that can be done with a bodiless voice.

What, indeed, is an acousmêtre in a film? It can be a Master who speaks behind a curtain, like Pythagoras. But it is also:

someone who is mistaken for someone else;
someone who does not say where he is speaking from (like
    on the telephone);
the voice of a dead person who speaks (as in *Sunset
    Boulevard*);
a prerecorded voice coming from a mechanical device;
or even the voice of a Machine-Being.

The Testament racks up all these possibilities of the acousmêtre, and it does not bother about the logical contradictions that pile up in consequence.

Ultimately it would appear that Mabuse is nothing—nothing more or less than what people construct him as—and that he can exist at all because none of his properties is fixed. If there is a Mabuse, he is in this name without an identity, this body without a voice, this voice without a place; in the general madness of these dis-assembled elements, he is all possible acousmêtres and none at all, and when all is said and done, an *acousmachine*.

THE QUEST FOR THE ACOUSMACHINE   Let us pick up on *The Testament of Dr. Mabuse* at the crucial moment when Kent unmasks the mechanism simulating the Chief. He and Lily have just been locked into this room as punishment (he disregarded the Chief's orders).

> MABUSE'S VOICE: Kent! You were ordered to make preparations for the attack on the bank. You have not obeyed. Disobedience is treachery. This means death for both of you.
> KENT: Let this woman go! Do whatever you want with me, but let the woman go!
> THE VOICE: You and this woman will not leave this place alive.

Kent draws a gun and fires at the curtain. The room suddenly goes dark. Flashes in the darkness. We don't know what side of the curtain we're on. Are we behind, facing Kent and Lily, or out in front, seeing through their eyes? Then we hear the curtain rip, and Kent and Lily appear before us, stupefied by what they see before them. It's absolutely as if they were discovering reality—the movie theater and its audience.

A reverse shot reveals what they see, namely, the mechanical ap-paratus described above. Kent and Lily do not put into words what is before them; Lily only mutters, "Good God!" The voice continues as if nothing had happened, now coming out of the fully visible speak-er horn: "Neither of you will leave this room alive. Only three more hours and you will die." Then it stops for good, and only a quiet reg-ular ticking is heard, like a metronome. "Whatever it is," says Kent, "we must find it and put it out of action."

Writing about this ticking time bomb, Luc Moullet makes a sig-nificant error. He identifies it as the deafening sound of the invisible machine heard in the first scene of the film, when Hofmeister hides

Rudolf Schündler, Gustav
Diessl, and Wera Liessem....

...in the
curtained room of *The
Testament of Dr. Mabuse.*

in a room shaken by vibrations.[1] These two sounds are as different as they could be. The first is a loud and unceasing pounding or crashing, like a gigantic water pump, while the sound Kent and Lily hear is slight and discontinuous. But even in this memory lapse Moullet is nevertheless right in one respect. What these noises have in common is their implacable regularity and the same impossibility of *seeing the heartbeat* of the terrible acousmatic machine.

The acousmachine is born when the voice stops. It's as if the acousmêtre itself were becoming an acousmachine. The moment before, when the curtain served as an obstacle between the voice and us, the voice spoke or seemed to speak with Kent as a living being. Subsequently it seems to have seen and heard nothing of the fall of the curtain and the gunshot, and it continues to issue its threat like a parrot. Here the American print benefits from dubbing to change the meaning of the scene. "You stupid idiot!" says the voice, *reacting* to events, behaving like the voice of a living being. I find the *transition to automatism* in the original German version to be much stronger emotionally and more troubling, as it unveils the acousmêtre as a mechanism.

An elegant metaphor of film and of mise-en-scène is contained in this episode. What the couple finds in tearing down the barrier of the curtain is what the film spectator would find if he tried to take the projected image as a concrete material reality, if he tried to dismantle the barrier that ensures his belief in this fiction, if he were to tear apart the screen, *this curtain that conceals itself*—in order to enter the space of its false depth. What would he see? A loudspeaker and shadows (just as the cutout silhouette is a flat shadow), a mechanism, nothing living. In a way, Kent and Lily find themselves in a mechanical recording and replay. But no: the mechanism is before their eyes, they don't notice that they are implicated in it, any more than the spectator applies to her own film-viewing the disillusionment she sees in Kent and Lily when they realize that the acousmêtre is a recorded simulacrum. We witness their astonishment at something that we also desire to see: the Langian device of the 180-degree,

1. Moullet, *Fritz Lang*, in the
collection "Cinéma d'aujourd'hui"
(Paris: Séghers, 1963), p. 34.

42

direct-address reverse shot fulfills our desire and shows us what they see as they look toward us.

Here we come close to something that might be called the mirage of the absolute reverse shot—that the film's characters could see us as we see them, and that once they've seen us, we topple over into the screen. One of the first 180-degree reverse shots of the cinema, after all, can be found in a Griffith short about a theater show; what does this reverse shot show us but the spectators in the theater?

But what Kent and Lily see is a technical setup. The two characters remain deaf and blind to our auditorium because they are simulacra who don't know it. In much the same way, the talking acousmachine behaves like a projection, and remains deaf and blind to Kent and Lily's actions. The machinery alludes to Kent and Lily's own status as simulacra. It points as well to the situation of spectatorship, to film itself as a simulation (the curtain as obvious metaphor for the stage curtain). Which doesn't prevent Kent, Lily, and the spectator from continuing to "function" to the tune of "I know, but all the same . . . "

The other "voice machine" discovered at Baum's, the record with the repeating groove set in play by those who try to enter, is not an acousmachine. This mechanism is referred to by name, and is wholly inscribed in the visual field. On the other hand, in the room where Kent and Lily are locked in, it's quite clear that we will never see the nonexistent place whose existence is implied by the unveiled microphone and speaker. For if there is a mike, where does it feed to, and if there's a speaker, where is it outputting from? Nor will we see the central place where the bomb is hidden, and the machine that deafened Hofmeister. (One suspects that the latter machine is the counterfeiters' printing press seen in another scene, but the film is by no means conclusive.)

So the perfection of the acousmachine consists of the notion that its center cannot be reached, and it is impossible to defuse. In the stories of Edgar P. Jacobs, there is always an underground hideout, a central lair that Blake and Mortimer get to, the control center you must reach in order to deactivate the diabolical machinery.[2] In such a control center the couple in the last *Mabuse* will finally find themselves, thereby marking the end of the cycle (*The Thousand Eyes of Dr. Mabuse*). Meanwhile, the Mabuse of *The Testament* is not yet an "Olrik," and his acousmachine is not yet a control center tucked away somewhere with someone in command. It is a *sound*, an unlocalizable sound of operation. We may find in this an allegory of metronomic time, a representation of the dance of hours that leads to death. Also, perhaps, a figuration of bodily rhythms as heard from within, as the fetus would hear it. Think of the first appearance of Hofmeister, hunched over listening, while the giant acousmachine is throbbing in a rhythm that uncannily resembles an adult heartbeat. This acousmachine occupies no-place; it inhabits the all-around (what Didier Anzieu calls the "sonorous envelope") that precedes the subject's ability to distinguish discrete places.

A DEATH IN NO-PLACE   The main character of Kubrick's *2001* is the computer Hal, whose voice permeates the spaceship Discovery. Kubrick shows us one or two of the "eyes" with which Hal sees, just small red lenses, which supposedly exist in large numbers all over the ship. But Kubrick did not deem it necessary to insist visually on Hal's eye each time the computer speaks or has "seen" something. Why? Because Hal is first and foremost a voice; like Mabuse behind the curtain, he has eyes in his voice. It is a man's voice—steady, gentle, and impersonal—and Hal has only to inhabit the entire space of the ship with this voice in order to be understood as ubiquitous, all-seeing, all-knowing, and endowed with prodigious power. The beauty of *2001* derives as much from this economy of means as from its sublime special effects.

Once Hal gone berserk has eliminated all the other astronauts, how will Dave Bowman render Hal incapable of further destruction? By going inside the place that is the heart and brain of the acousmêtre.

The banal approach to depicting the demise of Hal would surely

2. [Jacobs was a British author of comic books in France. These adventure stories featured Black and Mortimer, agents of the British intelligence service, and the evil genius Olrik. *Trans.*]

have been to film explosions with lots of noise, smoke, cascading debris. Kubrick's solution is far more economical and expressive. Hal exists as a voice, and it's by his voice, in his voice, that he dies. As Dave disconnects his circuits (Hal begging him not to all the while), the voice changes, is undone, finally plunges grotesquely to the bottom like a record that slows and stops on the turntable. This downward slide toward silence, reinforced by the image of the red eye that goes out, makes for the most moving acousmêtre death in cinema.

But in the course of this agony, narrated live by Hal's pseudo-consciousness ("Dave, stop. Stop, will you? Stop, Dave . . . I'm afraid . . . Dave, my mind is going. I can feel it. My mind is going. . . . "), there is a precise moment of *shifting into automatism*. Just as upon the removal of the curtain-barrier the acousmêtre Mabuse becomes a mechanism, so too Hal changes from being a subject to a non-subject, from a living acousmêtre to an acousmachine. After his heartrending appeals, with no reverb, he abruptly changes tone and begins to spout, with the perked-up voice of a young computer, the patter he was taught "at birth": "Good afternoon, gentlemen. I am a HAL 9000 computer. . . . " From then on he is only a recording; he sings "Daisy, Daisy." As soon as he is quiet, another recording takes his place—not Hal—which discloses to Dave the goal of his mission.

It is remarkable that in 2001 as in *The Testament of Dr. Mabuse*, the switch from acousmêtre to acousmachine is an inscrutable and unthinkable moment which we can comprehend only by what goes before and after. There is no gradual transition from one to the other. The passage to automatism is also perhaps the moment when the image "peels off" from the living person. The living person dies so that the image that is pure mechanical recording may live, as in Poe's "Oval Portrait" or in Augusto Genina's little-known film *Prix de beauté*. In the latter, Louise Brooks plays a young movie star. Sitting in a screening room watching the first film she starred in, *La Chanteuse éperdue*, she is killed by her jealous husband. Upon her death, her film takes over the whole screen, as if the death of the original were allowing the mechanized simulacrum to fully come to life.

What is perhaps most troubling about the death of Hal the acousmêtre is that this death is no-place. The voice itself is the locus of the mechanism that leads to the acousmêtre's demise. The textual repetition of Mabuse's voice, taken over by the time bomb's ticking; the downward slide of Hal's voice . . . a strange death, leaving no trace, no body.

THE DEAD SPEAK "A real presence, perhaps, that voice that seemed so near—in actual separation! But a premonition also of an eternal separation! Many were the times, as I listened thus without seeing her who spoke to me from so far away, when it seemed to me that the voice was crying to me from the depths out of which one does not rise again, and I felt the anxiety that was one day to wring my heart when a voice would thus return (alone and attached no longer to a body which I was never to see again), to murmur in my ear words I longed to kiss as they issued from lips for ever turned to dust."[3]

This is how Proust, in *Remembrance of Things Past*, evokes the acousmatic voice of his grandmother heard over the telephone. Ever since the telephone and gramophone made it possible to isolate voices from bodies, the voice naturally has reminded us of the voice of the dead. And more than our generation, those who witnessed the birth of these technologies were aware of their funerary quality. In the cinema, the voice of the acousmêtre is frequently the voice of one who is dead. William Holden's voice in *Sunset Boulevard* narrates his own story up to the gunshot that sends him into the swimming pool face down; the voice "sees" its own body as a corpse being fished out of the pool by the living. There is the phantom-voice of Rex Harrison at the end of Mankiewicz's *The Honey Pot*, impotently commenting on the failure of his posthumous plans. And among many other examples, Maupassant's voice speaks over a black screen in Ophuls's *Le Plaisir*. The famous line from Poe's novella *The Strange Case of Mr Valdemar* is apt: "I tell you that I am dead." An oxymoronic statement, it seems to contain its own contradiction, and at the

3. Marcel Proust, *Du côté de Guermantes*, vol. 2 of *A la Recherche du Temps Perdu* (Paris: Pléiade ed., 1954), p. 134; C.K. Scott Moncrieff and Terence Kilmartin, trans., *The Guermantes Way* (New York: Vintage/Random House, 1982), p. 135.

46

same time it doesn't have the quality of an elegant paradox. Every-one understands immediately what it is saying.

What could be more natural in a film than a dead person contin-uing to speak as a bodiless voice, wandering about the surface of the screen? Particularly in the cinema, the voice enjoys a certain proxim-ity to the soul, the shadow, the double—these immaterial, detach-able representations of the body, which survive its death and some-times even leave it during its life.

When it is not the voice of the dead, the narrative voiceover is often that of the almost-dead, of the person who has completed his or her life and is only waiting to die.

Janet Leigh and Anthony Perkins in *Psycho* (Alfred Hitchcock, 1960).

THREE THE I-VOICE

Often in a movie the action will come to a standstill as someone, serene and reflective, will start to tell a story. The character's voice separates from the body, and returns as an acousmêtre to haunt the past-tense images conjured by its words. The voice speaks from a point where time is suspended. What makes this an "I-voice" is not just the use of the first person singular, but its placement—a certain sound quality, a way of occupying space, a sense of proximity to the spectator's ear, and a particular manner of engaging the spectator's identification.

The French term for the word "voiceover" is "voix-off" (as if any voice could be "off"), and it designates any acousmatic or bodiless voices in a film that tell stories, provide commentary, or evoke the past. *Bodiless* can mean placed outside a body temporarily, detached from a body that is no longer seen, and set into orbit in the peripheral acousmatic field. These voices know all, remember all, but quickly find themselves submerged by the visible and audible past they have called up—that is, in flashback.

Obviously the cinema didn't invent the narrating voice. Just as film appropriated the music of opera and orchestra pit in order to accompany its stories, it also integrated the voice of the *montreur d'images* or picture presenter, from a much older tradition. Jacques Perriault's book *Mémoires de l'ombre et du son* describes these lantern slide shows of fixed views that toured through the countryside in the eighteenth and nineteenth centuries, with texts designed to be read aloud; the programs were sometimes called "talking journals."

But we ought to go back even further. Since the very dawn of time, *voices have presented images*, made order of things in the world, brought things to life and named them. The very first image presenter is the mother; before the child learns any written signs, her voice articulates things in a human and linear temporality. In every master of ceremonies and storyteller as well as every movie voiceover, an aspect of this original function remains.

I have said that the point from which this cinematic voice speaks often seems to be a place *removed from the images*, away from the scene or stage, somewhat like the place occupied by the slideshow lecturer, the mountain climber commenting in person on his exploits.

As long as the film's voice speaks to us from this removed position of the picture-presenter, whether the narrator is physically present or recorded on the audio track, it does not differ essentially from the good old voice of the magic lantern show, the voice of the mother or father talking to the child they hold on their knees and who hears them overhead, their voices enveloping him like a big veil. The cinema might recall this strong and close presence of the parental voice, but perhaps on the other hand it causes us to lose opportunities for life, closeness, and the possibility of two-way communication.

The situation changes precisely when the voice is "engaged," to a greater or lesser degree, with the screen space, when the voice and the image dance in a dynamic relationship, now coming within a hair's breadth of entering the visual field, now hiding from the camera's eye. Think of the voice of Welles in the last shot of *The Magnificent Ambersons*: the microphone that appears in the empty screen points to the offscreen place where this narrator is speaking from. Were he to make the small step onscreen and reveal himself, this voice would play a significantly different role than that of a classical voiceover narrator. Between the point where the voice is "hiding out" and the point where it hazards its way into the image, there is no well-defined continuity; the slightest thing can make it tip one way or the other.

An I-voice is not simply an offscreen narrator's voice. Sound film has codified the criteria of tone color, auditory space, and timbre to which a voice must conform in order to function as an I-voice. These criteria are in fact full-fledged norms, rarely violated: dramatic norms of performance, technical norms of recording. They are far from arbitrary. If a film violates only one of them, we sense something amiss with the narration.

The cinematic I-voice is not just the voice that says "I," as in a novel. To solicit the spectator's identification, that is, for the spectator to appropriate it to any degree, it must be framed and recorded in a certain manner. Only then can it function as a *pivot of identification*, resonating in us as if it were our own voice, like a voice in the first person.

Two technical criteria are essential for the I-voice. First, *close miking*, as close as possible, creates a feeling of intimacy with the voice, such that we sense no distance between it and our ear. We experience this closeness via the surefire audio qualities of vocal *presence* and *definition*, which manage to remain perceivable even in the worst conditions of reception and reproduction, even through the low-fidelity medium of the telephone.

The second criterion derives from the first: "dryness" or absence of reverb in the voice (for reverb situates the voice in a space). It's as if, in order for the I-voice to resonate in us as our own, it can't be inscribed in a concrete identifiable space, it must be its own space unto itself. All you have to do is add reverb in the mix to manipulate an I-voice; the *embracing* and *complicit* quality of the I-voice becomes *embraced* and *distanced*. It is then no longer a subject with which the spectator identifies, but rather an object-voice, perceived as a body anchored in space.

It's precisely this distinction that Hitchcock exploited with such finesse in *Psycho*. On one hand, there are the internal voices, object-voices that we understand to be heard by Marion during her drive to escape from Phoenix. On the other, there's the voice that's called internal but is really a subject-voice—I-voice—that belongs to the mother at the end of the film, superimposed on the images of a silent Norman sitting in his cell.

In the first of these two scenes, Marion (Janet Leigh) is at the steering wheel and is concocting a whole internal drama on what various characters she has spoken to must be saying: the head of the bank, her fellow secretary, and the millionaire whose money she has stolen. Their acousmatic voices, worried and then indignant, are heard over the image of Marion's face as she drives, as well as over shots of the monotonous highway landscape. How do we understand that these voices resonate "in her head," and not that they are voices calling up images of her as they talk about her? Because they conform to audio conventions that establish a sound as subjective, making it unrealistic. Which is exactly the opposite of an I-sound, since a "subjective" perception in a film is *objectivized* as such. In *Psycho*, the technical manipulations consist of a pronounced filtering, which makes the voices resemble telephone voices, as well as addition of reverb which incorporates them into an imaginary place, the place of her head, her imagination. Suppose we were able to take the elements of the mix, and edit the same voices to the same images but take away filters and reverb, so that the voices had the presence of an auditory closeup. I'd bet that there would be a completely different effect. No longer contained, the voices would now contain and order the image. Instead of their coming across as Marion's inner hearing, the face of Marion might well be seen as the image evoked by the voices.

The second scene in question shows Norman (Anthony Perkins) sitting in his cell wrapped in a blanket, his face "neutral" like Marion's, while the voice of the mother reels off a paranoid monologue. Internal voice of Norman, who we've been told identifies totally with his mother? More than that. The voice is close up, precise, immediate, without echo, it's an I-voice that vampirizes both Norman's body and the entire image, as well as the spectator herself. A voice that the image is inside of.

Note the parallel between the two scenes: same closeups of silent, rather expressionless faces, and same overlay, onto these faces of acousmatic voices. Nonetheless the voices function in opposite ways. The internal voices that fascinate Marion resonate in her head, whereas the embracing voice that speaks over the image of Norman resonates in us. It's a voice in exile,[1] it cannot be reintegrated either into the dried mummy discovered in the basement, or into the inappropriate body of Norman Bates, this living body of her son whom she possesses from now on, unless somehow he were to master it in himself, circumscribe it, impose limits on it.

1. [Chion's term here is *en souffrance de corps*: awaiting delivery of a body, with a body on back order; but it also carries the connotation of a body suffering, that something is missing. For an extended discussion, see chapter 9. *Trans.*]

52

We might call this an effect of *corporeal implication*, or involve- ment of the spectator's body, when the voice makes us feel in our
body the vibration of the body of the other, of the character who
serves as a vehicle for the identification. The extreme case of corporeal implication occurs when there is no dialogue or words, but only
closely present breathing or groans or sighs. We often have as much
difficulty distancing ourselves from this to the degree that the sex,
age, and identity of the one who thus breathes, groans, and suffers
aren't marked in the voice. It could be me, you, he, she.

For example, at the end of *2001*, there is the breathing of Dave,
the escaped astronaut; we perceive it as loudly and immediately as he
hears it inside his space suit—and yet we see him lost in the inter-
planetary void like a tiny marionette. But this breathing manages to
make of this faceless, faraway puppet, floating in the void or in the
middle of machines, a *subject* with whom we identify through audi-
tive mimesis.

The effect of corporeal implication also occurs in David Lynch's
Elephant Man, in the scene where the elephant man is first ushered
into Dr. Treeves's office. The monster still has his mask on and we
haven't yet seen his features. He stands paralyzed before the doctor
who presses him with questions. But we hear his breathing and his
painful swallowing, with a presentness that only he could also hear,
and we feel his fear in our own body. This is an example of a scene
whose point of view is created entirely by sound. This farthest limit
of the I-voice doesn't even involve a voice (the elephant man hasn't
spoken), but of a pre-vocal expression, even before the air in the airway rattles the larynx. . . .

THE MASTER OF THE HOUSE   Thus, in order to take possession of the spectator and the images and even the characters, the voice has to avoid
that which designates it as a tangible object. Otherwise the spectator
would become conscious of the identification process by perceiving
its contours, its identity. Pascal Bonitzer characterized this effect of
"dis-illusion" or distancing of the I-voice: "To encounter the body of

the voice (its grain, as Barthes puts it), this physical chaff of meaning, is to encounter . . . the subject fallen to the status of object, un-
masked . . . so that we end up *hearing* this voice."[2] To avoid being thus
encountered as a body, the voice must, as I have said, move to the
foreground, without reverb. It must also not be *projected*—contrary
to public speech which in order to be effective must resonate in the
space the orator is addressing.

Why, in the films of Sacha Guitry and Jean Cocteau, are the directors' voiceovers so noteworthy in this respect? Their voices, even while
assuming the classical role of narrator or I-voice, break convention in
flaunting their singularity, and as *projected voices*. Instead of speaking
neutrally and pretending not to know it speaks to an auditorium,
the unusual acousmêtre of Cocteau himself in *Les Enfants terribles* or
Guitry in *Le Roman d'un tricheur* is overtly aware of its elocution, its
articulation, its timbre, the *distance* that separates it from us. Although
this acousmêtre might say "I," it still doesn't permit us to identify with
it. Cocteau's voice in Melville's *Les Enfants terribles* sounds more like an
author giving a speech than like the ordinary movie narrator. The
same goes for Guitry's which addresses us in a declamatory fashion, as
if to hear itself speak. The voice does not allow itself to be assimilated
as an internal voice or even an everyman's voice. A certain neutrality
of timbre and accent, associated with a certain ingratiating discretion,
is normally expected of an I-voice. Precisely so that each spectator can
make it his own, the voice must work toward being a *written text that
speaks* with the impersonality of the printed page.

If we hear a voiceover listening to itself talk, the image of a body
and of a person gets in the way of identification. It palpably takes its
seat between the image and us; instead of leading us into the image,
it sticks us onto it. The false cinematic I-voices of Cocteau and Guitry are a strange phenomenon. At the same time that they carry the
narration, they weigh it down with their corpulent presence. You
have to get by them to enter into the story, but they won't let you go,
like an indiscreet Master of the House who insists on accompanying
you everywhere you move.

2. Bonitzer, *Le regard et la voix*,
p. 42–43.

54

THE DAY THE ACOUSMÊTRES DOUBTED   The day the acousmêtres had doubts, when they no longer behaved like voices that knew and saw everything . . . Can we pinpoint when that happened in film history? Can't we say that alongside commanding, intimidating, all-seeing acousmêtres in the sound cinema, there has always been another species of doubting acousmêtres, deprived of thorough and omniscient knowledge? Sternberg's voice in *The Saga of Anatahan* is of this sort, with its way of saying "we" and its partial knowledge in relation to the images it accompanies. Such voices are still not codified to this day; they seem to have no clear status. What we can say at this point is that a kind of detour in the voiceover as the representation of the Other's / Master's knowledge can be detected in a number of films since the 1970s.

In Bertolucci's film *Tragedy of a Ridiculous Man*, the internal voice of the main character Primo elicits doubt—the more perversely so since it was added onto the soundtrack by the director largely after the fact, ostensibly to clarify but in reality to complicate.[3] No doubt the voice makes it plain that the story is from Primo's point of view (since a character's internal voice in a scene he appears in does place the scene in his perspective). But by being heard over images this "narrator" couldn't have seen, the voice produces a more disconcerting effect than with Sternberg. At least in *Anatahan* we know what the voiceover pretends not to know or really doesn't know. With Bertolucci the boundaries—and even the object—of this knowledge are completely obscured.

We might speculate that the "blind" voice or the voice with partial sight may be the voice of the excluded third party of the primal scene. Excluded isn't the right word, because the primal scene exists *only for that person*, who is at the heart of it. I'm thinking of Marguerite Duras and her *Ravishing of Lol V. Stein*, the matrix of a whole series of literary and filmic works with blind or semi-blind voices who do not see or know all. The phenomenon usually involves women's voices, while (it must finally be said) *most acousmêtres are masculine.* Female acousmêtres in classical cinema are rare—for

3. See "Entretien avec Bernardo Bertolucci" in *Cahiers du cinéma*, no. 330 (December, 1981), pp. 24–33.

55

example in Mankiewicz's *Letter to Three Wives*; even here, the wives' voices are also in the third person with respect to the husband and the "other woman."

On the other hand, some more recent permutations of the voiceover in films ranging from Terence Malick's *Days of Heaven* to Claude Lelouch's *Les Uns et les autres*, convey a man's side (even though the voice in *Days of Heaven* is that of a young girl) in the way they perturb the acousmêtre's customary omnivoyance and mastery, and derive perverse effects from doing so.

In *Days of Heaven*, the voiceover again belongs to a third party, the outsider to a couple—the hero's younger sister. Her voice plays an unusual game of hide-and-seek in terms of her knowledge about the adult world of sexual relations and violence. (In his debut feature, *Badlands*, Malick had already attempted to bring new poetic power to the voiceover, breaking conventions of narration to destructure the spectator's point of view.) In Lelouch, the voiceover is more naively twisted, so to speak, in its relation to the narrative. The author-director had one of his actors, Francis Huster, not only play his on-screen role, but record the film's explanatory commentary, as well as speak the credits aloud, and even overlay simultaneous translations of sequences in foreign languages (i.e., in scenes with letters being read), and even provide the voice that emerges from loudspeakers in concentration camp scenes! Rarely has there existed a film voice so entirely dispossessed of a place; the least we can say is that it serves as an all-purpose acousmêtre.

Why would this diversion, or even degeneration, of narration be more marked in the position of the voiceover than in any other narrative element? Precisely because the voiceover is constitutive of the narrative's *subject*—in the double sense of "what happens" and of "whom it happens to"—because it asks the question of the knowledge and desire of this subject, of its/his *point of view*. For very different reasons in the films of Bertolucci, Malick, and Lelouch, the place from which the acousmêtre speaks, the authority or the desire that it/he embodies, are all messed with, perturbed, to some extent.

This isn't by chance, but really a sign of the times, an era when telling a story exposes the teller more than it used to. These three directors may be making crafty attempts to "hide the story they tell," to cite the excellent phrase of Uziel Peres.[4]

All this issues from a "bizarre" period of the cinema in which we have witnessed a marked increase in the number of films, stories, and directors that juggle their options. And let's not forget those like Raul Ruiz, who are proposing really new solutions, other than what is dictated by habit and convention. A film like *The Hypothesis of the Stolen Painting*, in its manner of parodying the Master-of-the-House-like tone of voiceover commentators, and of playing two voices, two knowledges against each other, is overtly built on a subtle play with the traditional position of the acousmêtre, and it invites the spectator openly and frankly into the game.[5] More and more frequently the acousmêtre is becoming a complicated, calculating being. The cinema of each period gets the acousmêtre it deserves.

4. [Uziel Peres is an Israeli filmmaker who in the '70s and '80s directed melodramas inspired by Sirk and Chabrol. *Trans.*]

5. On this film, see *Le Champ aveugle*, Pascal Bonitzer, ed. (Paris: Cahiers / Gallimard), pp. 107 ff.

II. TAMAKI: TALES OF THE VOICE

Karl Meixner in *The
Testament of Dr. Mabuse.*

FOUR THE VOICE CONNECTION

THE UMBILICAL WEB   In the beginning, in the uterine darkness, was the voice, the Mother's voice. For the child once born, the mother is more an olfactory and vocal continuum than an image. Her voice originates in all points of space, while her form enters and leaves the visual field. We can imagine the voice of the Mother weaving around the child a network of connections it's tempting to call the *umbilical web*. A rather horrifying expression to be sure, in its evocation of spiders—and in fact, this original vocal connection will remain ambivalent.

The book by Denis Vasse entitled *The Umbilicus and the Voice* develops a theory grounded in his clinical experience of psychotic children and adults. At first glance this theory seems absurd—positing a primal relationship between the voice and the umbilical cord. First he locates, in psychotic structures, the role of the umbilicus as a Lacanian *"objet (a),"* as a "point of fixation . . . obturating object and reifying object of difference," in order then to link this object to the function of the voice, taken not solely "in the materiality of a phonematic object" (where it is itself reified as an *"objet (a)"*), but also—and here is Vasse's originality—"in its capacity as a nonobjectifiable medium of difference."

The umbilical zone, as a wound, "in its opaque materiality . . . inscribes at the very center of the infant the mark of desire . . . that he experiences as a member of his species." This desire perforce becomes, consciously or not, "implicated in the act of the cutting of the umbilicus." This act of "closing off" at birth "correlates strongly with the attention paid to the opening of the mouth and the uttering of the first cry." Thus, "the voice is inscribed in the umbilical rupture." By means of this closing "testifying, at the center of the body, to the definitive rupture from another body. . . . The child is assigned to reside in that body. . . . From then on, bodily contact with the mother becomes mediated by the voice." The umbilical cord and the voice thus constitute a pair in which "the umbilicus means closure, the voice is subversion of closure. Whether it names or calls, the voice traverses closure without breaking it in the process. On the contrary, the voice *signifies* closure as the place of a subject that cannot be reduced to corporeal localization. . . . All in a single act, it attests to the limit and escapes it."[1]

Denis Vasse doesn't say, but I am suggesting here, that the voice could imaginarily take up the role of an umbilical cord, as a nurturing connection, allowing no chance of autonomy to the subject trapped in its umbilical web. Clearly when the voice is heard separate from the body—i.e. in a regressive situation—it can play this role the most easily.

We can see this vocal connection represented in its vital, nurturing role at the beginning of *La Grande illusion*. Maréchal (Jean Gabin) leans on a gramophone speaker from which there emerges a woman's voice singing the old song "Frou-frou."[2] Women's absence from the first three-quarters of the film makes them all the greater a focus of desire for the prisoners whose story is told in the film. But here a woman is present through this voice, which will remain—almost exclusively until the final episode with the farm woman played by Dita Parlo—the sole female voice ever heard. It seems that Maréchal, shown a bit further into the film to be a ladies' man, is literally being nurtured by this voice, unaware at the moment that it's feeding him the necessary energy to carry him through the long captivity ahead.

Another famous image of a "vocal cord" in Renoir occurs at the beginning of *La Règle du jeu*. The female radio journalist reports into her microphone live from the crowded scene of Jurieu's plane landing at the airstrip; so again it is a woman's voice relayed by this cord. There is a relationship to be pointed out between the vocal connection, umbilical cords, and telephone cords.

PHONE STORIES One might think—not without naiveté—that it is the talking cinema that gave birth to stories built around telephones. We have only to see old silent films—including the early Griffith shorts—to dispel this notion. The telephone, and everything having to do

1. Denis Vasse, *L'Ombilic et la voix: deux enfants en analyse* (Paris: Editions du Seuil), 1974.
2. [A well known turn-of-the-century French song, its lyrics allude to the sound of women's skirts—"frou-frou" is onomatopoetic: "(Frou-frou, frou-frou) with her skirts the woman (frou-frou, frou-frou) disturbs men's souls . . ." *Trans.*]

with the circulation of sounds and voices, was as interesting to silent film as it was a challenge to depict.

Take for example a Griffith short from 1909, *The Lonely Villa*. The scenario is based on suspense via telephone, providing the occasion for parallel editing, a structure so dear to Griffith. A woman besieged in her country house by thieves telephones her husband, who is in town, and begs him to hurry home. The conversation is shown in crosscutting. This film proves that the voice doesn't necessarily have to be heard in order to create a telephone suspense sequence. Quite to the contrary, it's enough for the voice to be signified by the moving lips of the actors in the image.

Why is the telephone a favorite device of suspense narrative? Because it serves in separation and disjunction; the voice travels through space, bodies stay where they are. The phone scene encourages parallel editing, which as Pascal Bonitzer emphasizes, is one of the original figures if not the figure of suspense. In addition, it can have the effect of "suspending" a character we see from the voice of someone we don't see, who thereby gains all the powers of an acousmêtre.

Just as the intervention of an acousmatic voice often makes the story into a quest whose goal is to anchor the voice in a body, the voice of a stranger on the phone poses the necessity of localizing the source of the call, i.e. the voice's point of origin, and thus assigning a place to the voice that doesn't yet have one—and then, putting a face to this voice. For when the voice is not localized, it tends to suffuse the whole filmic space, and to take on terrifying powers.

A telephone is the opposite of a silent movie, in that it gives us a voice without letting us see who is speaking. This, too, accounts for its usefulness in narrative film. It even brings to the acousmatic situation a *vocal intimacy* that is rarely encountered in social life, for ordinarily you do not permit just anybody to speak right into your ear. The acousmatic phone caller, the threatening and perverse stranger (who, in film narratives, and doubtless also in reality, is most often a man), can adopt the powers of the acousmêtre, telling you he can see everything, knows everything, and is omnipotent. Inasmuch as you can't locate him, you can't figure out whether he's bluffing. No need here to list all the horror films that play on this dimension of the telephone.

A few examples will suffice. In Fred Walton's *When a Stranger Calls*, the power of the screenplay lies in the idea—taken from a newspaper article—that the stranger is phoning, without letting on, from the very house in which his victim—a babysitter played by Carol Kane—receives his messages; she thinks he is everywhere else, but certainly not there. When she becomes aware that her unseen persecutor is there, the entire space of this house, which she has been considering her only refuge, becomes inhabited by the presence of the voice. Horror and shock are virtually guaranteed when the voice we thought was elsewhere inhabits the familiar space or body.

In Fellini's *City of Women*, the presence of a phone in two or three places where Snaporaz (Marcello Mastroianni) goes indicates the weight of unseen eyes that follow him everywhere, even when he thinks he's alone. In the hotel of the feminist convention as well as in the narrow hallway on the way to the final arena and boxing ring, a phone rings, a woman picks up and answers someone whose voice we never hear: "He's here, I see him." The panoptic gaze is, like that of Mabuse or Hal, indicated far more effectively by this little game of mise-en-scène than if eyes were scattered everywhere.

When you write or direct a phone scene in a film, you must choose among several options. If for example you keep your camera on just one side of the conversation, you already have the choice of whether to let your audience hear the person on the other end of the line. We might call that character the *tele-locutor*, and the character we see the *proxi-locutor*. (Of course if the conversation is shown in crosscutting, proxi-locutor and tele-locutor constantly change place.) The classic suspense situation, used at the beginning of *When a Stranger Calls* and also in the 1950s version of *The Man Who Knew Too Much* as well as in many other phone stories, often avoids the crosscutting that would show who is speaking and where, and it leaves us on the side of the victim while we still hear this phone-voice that the victim is supposedly the only person to hear. Which is a way to make us share in the situation, and reinforce our identification.

On the other hand, a phone conversation in which the spectator remains with one of the characters but does not hear the voice of the tele-locutor, generally works against identification. It puts us in the position of a third party or visitor. This is also the effect produced when a character with whom we identify is present as a third party to a phone conversation. Such is the case in *Psycho* where, in the presence of Sam and Lila (the latter being our anchor for identification at the time, since her sister is dead), the sheriff phones Norman whose voice we don't hear during the call. (In many recent films, characters listen to music on their Walkmans, which the spectators also hear; we are surprised when a director like Rivette in *Le Pont du Nord* adopts an alternate strategy by depriving us of the music heard by the main character).

We could amuse ourselves by working out an entire typology of telephonic figures in film, classifying them according to whether the camera follows one side or both, one side or both in the audio, in crosscutting or in split screen. But we wouldn't be able to interpret in a predictable way each of these choices according to some definite effect it would produce, or the perspective it would establish on the fictional world. It is perfectly possible for the character who anchors identification to speak on the phone and for us to hear nothing of what the character hears.[3] Cocteau's play, *La Voix humaine*, filmed by Rossellini, is entirely written in this way. It distances us from the abandoned woman alone on stage, who talks on the phone with her lover who is leaving her and whose voice we never hear. And what to say about the telephonic figure we've encountered a thousand times—a prostrate character has just been killed, and from the receiver hanging near the body's ear we hear a voice calling in vain? The effect of death is indeed signified by its opposite; we hear the voice that the corpse can no longer hear.

3. For example *North By Northwest* has no consistent strategy. We do not hear Cary Grant's mother's voice as a tele-locutor when he phones her twice. But when he receives a call from one of the killers in "Kaplan's" room, which he is searching, then we do hear the killer's voice.

65

The use of the acousmatic voice of a phone call to suspend narrative action has rarely been as intelligently and efficiently exploited as in Sidney Lumet's *Fail Safe*. As a result of a botched radio transmission, an American bomber automatically receives the order to fly toward Moscow to drop his A-bombs on the Russian capital. The American president (Henry Fonda) must try to convince the Russians of his good faith over the phone, by trying everything in his power to intercept his own planes. Lumet never shows the adversaries. The Russians are purely acousmatic telephone voices that reach the president and his interpreter as the two are cooped up together in a room. Any aspect of these disembodied voices might be crucial. Everything hangs on the rightness of the translator's interpretation—not just the literal words, but also inflections, details between the lines. On the basis of this they must figure out the disposition of the tele-locutors. All the possibilities of entrapment and doubt inherent in the voice are present. Here the stakes of truth at the heart of speech, in its very failings and lapses, engage the fate of the world. The acousmatic vocal connection is stretched to the extreme with the greatest possible consequence if there's a misunderstanding: apocalypse.

DON'T HANG UP! In *The Testament of Dr. Mabuse*, there is a minor character whose function remains a mystery, but who seems instrumental in unifying the insane structure of the narrative. Hofmeister is a former policeman ousted from the force. Because he desperately wants to regain the respect of his superior, inspector Lohmann, he is pursuing some leads on a case of counterfeiting. It's in the course of this activity that he hears *a name* spoken, that of the man behind the whole affair, but many adventures and turns of plot will occur before he pronounces this name that burns his lips.

Hofmeister could have been a main character of *The Testament*, in that the story begins with him. However, he plummets into insanity, and his madness keeps him blocked in inaction. But just as the film began with him, it ends with him as well. Anyone who has seen *The*

Karl Meixner, Otto
Wernicke, and Klaus Pohl
in *The Testament of
Dr. Mabuse.*

Testament cannot forget the first scene, where in a basement trembling with the monstrous noise of some kind of machine, this character Hofmeister hides, curled up like a fetus. A door opens, and through it we get an even louder blast of the "acousmachine," indicating to us the direction to go to find the thing. Two men in white lab coats enter talking to one another. Because of the noise of the machines, we can't hear their voices, as if this were still a silent film. From the outset, Hofmeister is therefore associated with extreme auditory tension. The acousmachine with its gigantic noise, ever invisible; the impossibility of hearing what the men are saying; and this exploratory tracking shot through space, as if the camera is looking for the machine—everything conspires to create an auditory tension rarely equaled in the cinema.

The two men find Hofmeister, but they exit pretending not to have seen him. He emerges from his hiding place and goes frantically to listen at the door through which he is trying to escape. Later, escaping the trap laid to eliminate him, he hides in an office and, ever in danger, phones the police station to speak to Lohmann and reveal the name. The inspector has been trying to leave to go to the opera, and he refuses at first to listen to this "scoundrel." After a second very urgent call, Lohmann finally consents to take the phone. The conversation between the two men is shown in parallel editing, and we never hear one of the two voices as a telephone voice—except, precisely at the end, when Lohmann's receiver resonates with the piercing singing of Hofmeister who has gone insane. It is for this moment that Lang has reserved the acousmatic effect.

HOFMEISTER: I beg you, for the love of God, he has to listen to me, tell him that it's a matter of life or death!
MULLER *(Lohmann's secretary, to Lohmann)*: Commissioner, I think you absolutely must . . .
LOHMANN *(furious)*: Of course, I'm going to miss the first act! *(He takes the phone.)* This is Lohmann; what's going on?
HOFMEISTER *(transformed)*: Commissioner! I . . . I . . . I . . . thank you.
LOHMANN: Cut the small talk! Tell me what's going on.

HOFMEISTER (*comes to himself*): Yes, Commissioner. I . . . (*he stops, jumps at an invisible and inaudible threat, and wipes his fore head*): Just a second, please . . . Only in case . . . Commissioner, you must record my statement.

LOHMANN (*to Muller*): Pick up a phone, take notes!

HOFMEISTER: I . . . I wanted to be redeemed in your eyes, Commissioner, for four days, I've been watching . . . and now, I know who's behind all this.

LOHMANN: So who is it?

HOFMEISTER: I know who's behind it, the man behind the curtain, you'll think I'm crazy, I swear to you I'm telling the truth, I heard the name with my own ears! (*He stops*)

LOHMANN: Hofmeister, Hofmeister, God in heaven!

(*Shot of the telephone. We hear offscreen a sort of dull thud.*)

HOFMEISTER's voice (*a high wail, in the receivers of Lohmann and Muller*): Gloria, Gloria, schön sind die Mädel von Batavia . . .

(*A little later, Hofmeister is found to have gone insane.*)

Note that Hofmeister does not reveal at once all he has to say. He stalls as much as he can before giving his revelation, as if to *maintain the connection.* "He must listen to me," is his demand. A name he heard with his own ears is his discovery. Don't hang up, don't sever the auditory connection, that is his plea. And to remind us of this threat, on the desk where he telephones from, lies a figurine of a crocodile with its mouth open full of teeth, strategically aimed at the phone cord.

Insane after what has happened to him (we never find out what it was), Hofmeister takes refuge in the hallucinatory repetition of the phone scene. When he thinks he's alone in his cell, he sits in a sort of fetal position, trying to contact Lohmann on an imaginary phone. Subjective shots show his hallucinatory world wherein reality has the transparency of glass; the castrating crocodile itself has been transformed into a glass creature shouting with wide open maw. And the phone no longer has a cord.

As soon as he senses he is being watched, Hofmeister instantly quits the imaginary phone, and stares at his intolerable vision while singing "Gloria, Gloria" in a shrill falsetto. Why such a high pitch? Probably in order to have the reassuring hallucination of the voice that cradled him when he was little. For him, reality is contaminated by fantasy, and the only way to hook up with the real is imaginary— the telephone connection with Lohmann, upon which he pins all his hopes. He cannot stand either being seen or touched. He is henceforth reachable solely through the channel of the voice. It is difficult to imagine a more radical regression.

Therefore he cannot recognize Lohmann or speak to him. But as soon as he thinks Lohmann has left, he again takes up his position of phone fetus: "Commissioner Lohmann! Commissioner Lohmann!" By a stroke of intuition, Lohmann figures out how to enter his game. Standing by Hofmeister without being seen, Lohmann simulates the phone's ringing with his alarm clock (whose hands he must turn back, as if to go back in time to zero). "Hello! Lohmann here, who is it, please?" Hofmeister, transfigured with joy, answers right away. But when Lohmann makes a move toward him, he turns around and sees Lohmann, and at once, begins intoning his "Gloria" again. Later, Hofmeister has been given up for lost and is locked up in the asylum of Baum, who assigns him to the cell of Mabuse who died that very morning. He isn't seen again until the end. Baum, possessed and guided by the ghost of Mabuse, returns to the hospital, enters Hofmeister's cell and speaks to him. "Allow me to present myself. My name is Mabuse, Dr. Mabuse." What happens then so that upon hearing the name Hofmeister repeats it and shouts, like a shout of delivery, of aural childbirth? There too, as at the moment of trauma, the camera looks elsewhere. It is in the hallway and jettisons what is happening to offscreen space. When Lohmann arrives on the scene, Hofmeister emerges from the cell carried by two attendants. He gives Lohmann a devastating look of love before finally revealing what the commissioner already knows, but which Hofmeister wasn't able to say: "The name of the man is Mabuse, Commissioner, Dr. Mabuse."

70

So this is the name that has been lodged in his throat since the mysterious incident in the office. Saying this name, and passing it on to someone else (just like Baum transferred it to him), is a sort of deliverance. But from what? In both his real and imaginary phone calls, Hofmeister never stopped filling up time with excuses, expressions of fear, thank-yous, circumlocutions, all the hemming and hawing that Lohmann was annoyed at him for; he did that as if to put off to the final possible moment the uttering of the name. Maybe because he thinks that's all he has to give, and that the uttering of the name will mean no one will want to listen to him any more, while it's the aural connection that he wishes to maintain. His request is in fact "listen to me" rather than "listen to what I have to tell you" and his double bind is to give his present to be redeemed, to be loved, but at the same time to retain with Mother/Lohmann the voice connection he gets by holding on to the name. It's as if he cannot accept that the word, the name, is something that must be exchanged, lost, in order to remain alive. Discourse that cannot accept this and which doesn't run the risk of losing the object in the symbolic relationship it establishes, this discourse is doomed to lose meaning and engagement, in a total de-realization of the world.

The film does not reveal what was done to Hofmeister, because the screenwriters most likely didn't know either. The important thing is that it not be said—neither the nature of the trauma, nor the inability of the authors to say it. Screenwriters can get hung up in a lacuna, a forgotten detail, an omission in their story, and from this will be born the story itself.

The Testament of Dr. Mabuse embodies in a striking way the active power of the not-said. How many times in this film is it not said what is happening, and how many times are people, things and events not named? Thus, the villains summoned by Mabuse never pronounce his name among themselves, they say "the chief" or "the doctor," but this interdiction never gets explained. The punishment inflicted on traitors by the terrible section 2-B is often evoked as the thing to fear most, but it is never stated or clearly shown. When Lily and Kent discover the machinery behind the curtain, they do not name it and actually never name it to anyone.

Not naming, in order to gain time and be able to keep talking, transforming the voice into a nurturing and continuous umbilical flow, but with no stakes in meaning—making possible loss and cutting-off—this is not just the malady of Hofmeister; it is the problem of the entire film, and the very project of the *Testament of Dr. Mabuse*.

The more you watch this film, the more obvious it appears that its screenplay is, from a rational point of view, a tapestry of illogic that only hangs together because of the not-said that covers it, and because the power of Mabuse himself as the principle of Evil, arises precisely from this not-said. He lives only thanks to the prohibition against naming and going-to-find-out.

The film hangs together only insofar as we spectators accept and plug up the logical holes that constitute it. The speed and virtuosity of its editing, the transition effects (for example, one scene ends with Hofmeister driven mad by someone, and the next scene starts with the image of Mabuse), work to bridge the incoherence of the succession of scenes since the principle of linking by contiguity, contact, and contagion, comes out of a kind of magical thinking, which does not bother about contradictions. Likewise, Mabuse's destructive plan, written in black on white in his Testament, his method for consolidating the Empire of Crime, is to strike fear by random terrorist acts that shortcut logical thought. So if there are in these acts some blind alleys, false leads, or contradictions, they are not a failing in this movie but on the contrary they're its very essence. There's a troubling but brilliant similarity between Mabusian thought and the film's structure. The film's structure simultaneously makes things visible to whomever wishes to see the functioning of this perverse logic.

And Hofmeister? He is the very embodiment of the blind-alley quality of the narrative. The revelation he announces at the beginning and which he delivers at the end tells us nothing. The name he wishes to supply is known in advance by the spectator, since it's in the title. Perhaps this deferred revelation has no other function than to say, "Don't hang up, there's something to tell you!" Hofmeister serves to keep a seat warm at the asylum, between the dead Mabuse who had just left the very cell he occupies and Dr. Baum, who will return there and identify himself as Mabuse, displacing Hofmeister from it and delivering him from it at the same time. But this narrative function is a blind alley in itself, i.e., it's something that has no other role than to make us hold on. With the reference to the Master in his very name (etymologically the Master of the farm, or of the court), Hofmeister holds Mabuse's hand on one side, and Baum's on the other; he makes everything hold together with nothing, through the means of the not-said.

This character represents to himself alone, by his obstinate retention of Mabuse's name, the film's desire to keep the connection with the audience going. It is no accident that he is also the film's most regressive character, presented from the start as a *listening-being*.

A listening-being, but a certain kind of listening: that which reifies the flow of the voice into a connection deprived of meaning, in which nothing can be said other than phatic material.[4] "Hello, hello, Commissioner!" These repeated phrases say nothing more than "I'm speaking to you, don't hang up." For Hofmeister a word is either all or nothing, a risk he can't run, so he keeps it all for himself. For what does the telephonic fetus hang onto, if not to the voice as the cord that transmits a blind nurturing flow? The voice here is no longer "subversion of umbilical closure" (in Denis Vasse's formulation), but a foreclosure of closure, and paying for this foreclosure the price of non-sense and terror.

This, then, is what happens when you take a voice for an umbilical cord.

4. [Roman Jakobson describes the phatic function of language as establishing communication itself. An example is the words "Testing, one, two, three" spoken into a microphone. *Trans.*]

73

Jennifer Salt in *Sisters* (1972) and John Travolta in *Blow-Out* (1981), two films by Brian de Palma.

FIVE THE SCREAMING POINT

A woman is taking a shower. Someone rips open the shower curtain, waving a knife. Dramatic pause, then the woman screams her head off. We can easily recognize Hitchcock's *Psycho*, de Palma's *Blow-Out*, and countless other horror films. Since the cinema first discovered women screaming, it has shown great skill in producing screams and stockpiling them for immediate and frequent deployment.

This is why we can say that the plot of de Palma's *Blow-Out* is clearly rigged. It gives the viewer the mistaken impression that you can't find a good scream when you need one for a movie sequence like the one I've just described.

At the beginning of *Blow-Out* we are in effect watching the classic scene, shot with a subjective camera, showing the stalker who enters a bathroom, pulls a knife, throws open the shower curtain to reveal the woman . . . But the action stops there, for the scream that comes from the actress's mouth is a pathetic yelp. The lights go up in the screening room. It was a sex-and-violence movie, for which hero Jack (John Travolta) is supposed to provide the sound effects. The scream heard was what the actress herself produced during the take, and she wasn't cast for her terrific voice. It falls to Jack somehow to obtain a convincing scream to synch to the image. Meanwhile, the film in progress seems to stop at this point of suspense, before the knife's entry. That's how the plot of *Blow-Out* begins.

Actually Jack promptly forgets about the problem as he leaves work. He walks into the park at night with his Nagra, to augment his sound library with some nature sounds, especially wind—not to find a scream. An accident he witnesses and whose sound he happens to record draws him into a politics-gangsters intrigue. Getting involved despite some good advice to the contrary gives him the excuse to remain deaf to the appeals of his boss: "So when are you going to get me the scream?"

What is the flamboyant finale of *Blow-Out* leading up to, cleverly arranged so that everything—the Liberty Bell celebration, the great peal of church bells, a magnificent fireworks display, and the characters themselves—converges on the moment the killer slits the throat of Jack's girlfriend Sally? What is this prodigious narrative machine directed toward—where the entire sky is afire—if not the scream of the woman stabbed? Jack gets a recording of this scream, since he had wired Sally, supposedly for protection, with a micro-transmitter that allowed him to monitor and follow her.

This isn't Jack's first horrible mistake. In the past an investigator whom he had equipped similarly died because of him. Jack's unconscious has arranged once again for him to place Sally into a perilous position. The sole result is that he is enabled to record remotely from her mouth the scream he's been after (and which he "missed" with the investigator's death because of a technical difficulty). In a conventionally right-thinking film, the author would "hold on" to the scream in order to feed the emotion of his own story, as opposed to the story of the film-within-the-film. The honesty of de Palma's film lies in the notion that on the contrary, Jack will take this scream to his satisfied mixer ("now, that's a scream!"). This allows the film-within-the-film to be completed, after which *Blow-Out* itself just ends too, as if this whole intrigue were only a monstrous parasitic outgrowth around a professional anecdote, a duty the hero is endlessly trying to discharge.

In truth this scream, about whose credibility the characters make such a fuss, is less important as an object. What's more important is the *point* where it is placed in the story: it becomes a sort of ineffable black hole toward which there converges an entire fantastic, preposterous, extravagant mechanism—the celebration, the political crime, the sexual murder, and the whole film—all this made in order to be consumed and dissipated, in the unthinkableness and instantaneity of this scream.

So let us define the *screaming point* in a cinematic narrative as something that generally gushes forth from the mouth of a woman, which by the way does not have to be heard, but which above all must fall at an appointed spot, explode at a precise moment, at the crossroads of converging plot lines, at the end of an often convoluted trajectory, but calculated to give this point a maximum impact.[1] The film functions like a Rube Goldberg cartoon mechanism full of gears, pistons, chains and belts—a machine built to give birth to a scream.

I use the expression *screaming point* to emphasize that it's not so much the sound quality of the scream that's important, but its placement. And this place could be occupied by nothing, a blank, an absence. The screaming point is a point of the unthinkable inside the thought, of the indeterminate inside the spoken, of unrepresentability inside representation. It occupies a point in time, but has no duration within. It suspends the time of its possible duration; it's a rip in the fabric of time. This scream embodies a fantasy of the auditory absolute, it is seen to saturate the soundtrack and deafen the listener. It might even be unheard by the screamer.

In films like *Psycho*, the original *King Kong*, *The Man Who Knew Too Much*, *Blow-Out*, and part of *The Towering Inferno*, it's amazing to consider the extravagant luxury of the means devoted to the screenplay and production mobilized in order for everything to be lost and spent in a woman's scream. Nothing is spared in order to reach the screaming point. Twenty-story gorillas are invented, a thousand-foot-tall building is set ablaze, deluges of fireworks, symphony orchestras, the most ingenious and sophisticated details of production . . . For, in these films, at a certain moment, all disparate plot lines converge and break at this moment that quickly dissipates and passes, this moment of the woman's scream. As in the monstrous social rite of potlatch, nothing is too elaborate or far out if it will lead to a successful scream.

Why a woman's scream? Is this a phenomenon endemic to a cinema of sadists, who get off on the spectacle of a woman as prey to terror? Yes, but: we might also speculate that for men, the woman's scream poses the question of the "black hole" of the female orgasm, which cannot be spoken nor thought. In the very films that are

1. This notion can be applied to silent films as well as sound films.

77

constructed upon this scream as the absolute in terror and pleasure, the scream is not strongly eroticized, despite the frequently sadistic nature of the situation; this would tend to thwart the male climax. What it embodies, rather, is an absolute, outside of language, time, the conscious subject.

Why can't a man's scream give expression to this absolute just as well? This is what Skolimowski's aptly-named film *The Shout* tries to do. The film prepares us for quite a while to hear an awe-ful magic shout, the secret weapon of a sorcerer (or pseudo-sorcerer) played by Alan Bates. This shout occurs finally toward the end of the film. The director yelled it himself and then subjected it to electronic manipulation.

It is impressive, all right, but simply in a different league than the screaming point. The gender emphasis is already built in to the two terms in English for these wordless cries—we tend to call the woman's cry a scream, and the man's cry a shout. Skolimowski/Bates's cry is a shout of power, exercising a will, marking a territory, a structuring shout, *anticipated*. If the shout has something bestial to it, it's like the identification of the male with the totemic animal. The most famous example of this is Tarzan's call, fabricated in the 1930s from multiple animal cries; a phallic cry which the male uses to exhibit himself and proclaim his virility.

The woman's cry is rather more like the shout of a human subject of language in the face of death. The screaming point is of a properly human order. Perhaps Marguerite Duras has created the only exception, in having a man emit a scream that's neither a Tarzan's, nor a Beast's, nor a sorcerer's cry—the scream of the Vice-Consul in *India Song* and in *Son Nom de Venise*.

The screaming point, in a male-directed film, immediately poses the question of *mastery*, of the mastery of this scream.

The question of the means and power used to obtain the scream is posed outright in a famous scene in *King Kong* (1933). On a ship making its way toward Skull Island where the gorilla resides, a sadistic film director makes heroine Fay Wray try out some screams in a

78

screen test, prepping her by describing the horror of the monstrous beast. Usually where a filmmaker constructs a good story full of complications in order to draw things out to a screaming point, he makes sure to show how the screaming point can escape the very person orchestrating it in the story; the character can only give himself the illusion of being Master. With Hitchcock, de Palma, or in *King Kong*, it is clear that the man is but the organizer of the spectacle, the producer of this extravaganza, but that the screaming point ultimately is beyond him, just as it is beyond the woman who issues it as the medium.

The man's shout delimits a territory, the woman's scream has to do with limitlessness. The scream gobbles up everything into itself—it is centripetal and fascinating—while the man's cry is centrifugal and structuring. The screaming point is where speech is suddenly extinct, a black hole, the exit of being.

All of cinema, this omnivorous and diverse art, is thrown into the operation of this mechanism, this strategy of obtaining a screaming point in which the insane mobilization of resources justifies and even loses itself.

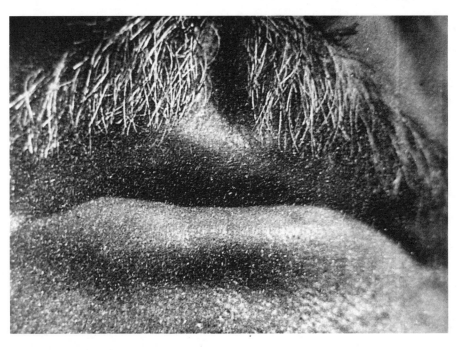

The mouth of Kane
(Orson Welles) saying
"Rosebud" (*Citizen Kane*,
Orson Welles, 1941).

SIX THE MASTER OF VOICES

JACQUES TATI'S "SILHOUETTE" VOICES   Anyone directing sound films must reckon sooner or later with being the Master of Voices. But in what respect is the voice something that must be mastered—or better yet, contained?

Since the dawn of the talkies people have been aware of the voice's capacity to dominate. It has a widely recognized tendency in film to *take up more space* than bodies. The concern for intelligible dialogue has traditionally led to the systematic recording of voices in auditory closeup, and their subsequent foregrounding in mixing as well, such that the voice is privileged over other soundtrack elements. These facets of recording and mixing have become such standard practice that when a director wishes for speech *not* to be clearly understood, but to be perceived as murmuring, chattering, or noise (e.g. in films of Ophuls, Tati, Fellini, Godard, Altman), the effort has often been met with enormous resistance by professionals, not to mention the audience. Sound engineers are afraid, with good reason, that a lack of intelligibility will be chalked up to technical ineptitude. For the audience's part, having their normal listening habits disrupted can be frustrating when they're unable to get the words.

The privileged position voices customarily enjoy on the soundtrack has the effect of bringing speaking characters "upstage." Even if we see them from afar, or lose track of them visually in some architectural setting, their proportionately louder and more present voices magnify them and bring them up close. In a famous deep-focus shot in *Citizen Kane*, Charlie Kane's mother in the foreground signs the papers sealing the destiny of her son. We see Charlie far in the background playing outside in the snow. What is it that makes us aware of this small figure, what never allows us to forget he's there during the entire scene? It's the kid's yelling as he plays a game ("The Union forever!"), these shouts that continuously mark his presence. If we were to remix *Kane* and delete Charlie's voice (which is, by the way, not necessary to the action—he could play silently, the window could be closed, the distance could prevent his voice from being heard), it's a sure bet that the small figure in the background, no matter how sharply focused, would be easier to forget about. This demonstrates how the presence or absence of a voice can give a character a greater or lesser dramatic weight.

When Jacques Tati applies unorthodox audio practices deliberately to give his characters rather weak, unintelligible voices, matching in audio scale the long shot he generally films in, he gets a uniquely perturbing effect. In his films, the voice is not an emphatic vehicle for text; the voice instead helps to shape the character's physical being, in much the same way as do the character's costume and physical behavior. And if we can compare the size of a voice to the visual space it "occupies," we may say that Tati's voices are always smaller than the shots they inhabit. The voice in Tati avoids dominating the image, and remains modestly in its place, circumscribed by the body that is fixed as its source. In order not to bring the character too far upstage, or to have the voice listened to too much for the meaning of the words, Tati even employs his own special tricks of dubbing and mixing.[1] For example, in mixing he creates slight audio fades, fluctuations of levels that make the voice "blink," prevent it from taking on too much body or authority. His technique also emphasizes the *music* of speech, with its accents, its peaks and rhythms, contributing to the voice's stylization.

So the human voice does not invade the entire acoustic space but rather allows plenty of room in the acoustic field, so that noise, which is usually in the background, can regain prominence and "speak" for itself.

With Tati you lose count of all the gags based on the animistic use of noises that make objects and machines talk. In *Playtime*, men sit on chairs that go "pfff"; the conversation in which they engage, as they rise and sit, is a conversation of "pfff"s. A multivehicle crash makes a car cluck like a hen. Windshield wipers snivel, squawk, grunt, or moan, depending on the personality of their owners. It's in

1. All sound in Tati's films is post-synched.

the context of this speechmaking of sounds that the human voice is subdued, restored to the level of a noise.[2]

Tati almost always uses sound *here and now*; things and bodies usually emit sound only during the time they appear in the image. The sound of a car that leaves the frame, in *Traffic*, is rapidly faded down. There is little offscreen sound other than ambient or environmental sound. When a noise poses the question of its source, the answer lies not in the next shot, but in the selfsame shot, hidden somewhere "in the painting" (like the anamorphic objects in Holbein's famous portrait of the ambassadors).

This implies that voices are not left to their "natural" bent, which is to occupy the scenic foreground. They must be contained. And it's no accident that this preoccupation with containing voices is manifested most patently in the French cinema. It's a veritable obsession, for example, in the films of Robert Bresson.

BRESSON: SUMMONING THE ANCESTOR   Bresson and Tati are often rightly associated for making brilliant use of sound, each in his own way. And it is true that for these two directors, the art of working with and exploiting sounds is consistent with a certain *retaining* of voices. Bresson's retention consists in the way he imposes a famously monotonous diction upon his actors—his "models" as he calls them. It's not so much the monotony of their delivery that seems to rattle the audience (and they really do get bothered) as the strangeness of its vocal production, such as had never been heard in movies or even in the theater. The Bressonian model speaks like we listen: by taking in, as he goes, what he has just said—so that he seems to be closing his mouth and ending his speech even as he is producing it, without leaving it the possibility of resonating for his interlocutor or the audience. This is clearly what Bresson meant when he advised his actors to speak "as if to themselves." Each word, each sentence, once uttered, forms a sort of island, irrevocably closed off. There is in Bresson a singular aversion to reverberation of voices in space, in the body of the other. He seems to hate the resonance created by a

2. See Michel Chion, *The Films of Jacques Tati*, Monique Vinas, Patrick Williamson, and Antonio d'Alfonso, trans. (Toronto: Guernica, 1997).

reverberant place like a church or a big room as much as the resonant effect created by some ways of speaking.

We see this aversion in *A Man Escaped*, a film about a resistance fighter's escape from prison. The story, taken from the memoirs of Commander Devigny, was admirably suited to Bresson's aesthetic.[3] For if most of the characters in this beautiful film talk "à la Bresson," avoiding any projection of the voice and hardly moving their lips, for once the plot actually justifies this strange diction—they are prisoners under constant surveillance, not allowed to speak. On the other hand, the jailers, the masters, the embodiments of evil, speak in a kind of barking, which makes the space of the prison resonate theatrically.

The phobia of reverb surfaces even more obviously in *The Devil Probably*. Serge Daney's writing on this film is a critical landmark on the subject of the voice in film.[4] In the church scene Daney analyzed, what is unusual is that the voices of those who speak aloud in the edifice do not resonate at all. Bresson thereby shows that he doesn't give a damn about auditory verisimilitude.[5]

By the time Bresson gets to *The Devil*, no voices resonate (except perhaps the recorded choral music of Monteverdi on the soundtrack) and all characters speak flatly, by which I mean both emotionlessly and with no reverb. On the other hand, as Daney notes, the sound is often "too loud." But what sound? At the beginning of the film, a *bateau-mouche* goes by on the Seine at night, its motor emitting a low muffled sound. We hear this deep, archaic sound as the voice of the Ancestor. It evokes the rhombus, an African ceremonial instrument used in certain magic traditions, precisely, to summon the Ancestor. This voice can also be heard in the extraordinary groans produced by trees cut down with chain saws (in the sequence of the environmental documentary), and in the rumbling of elevators. All these noises have a muted, dramatic, even deeply moving quality in the film. Are they voices of the Ancestor, who speaks without being heard in an insensate world? Or are they the voice of the Devil, because of whom, as Daney suggests, men take care not to open their mouths too wide, lest he dive in?

3. [Devigny was the French resistance fighter who recounted his escape from a Lyon prison in *Un Condamné à mort s'est échappé*, the book Bresson's film is very faithfully based on. His narrative is full of sonic details about life in prison under the Nazis and the collaborationist government of Pétain. *Trans.*]

4. Daney, "L'Orgue et l'aspirateur (La voix off et quelques autres)," *Cahiers du cinéma* no. 279–80 (Aug.-Sept, 1977), pp. 19–27. Another key text is Pascal Bonitzer's essays in his *Le Regard et la voix* (Paris: Union Générale d'Editions, 1976).

5. All voices in the scene are rerecorded in post-synch.

As early as Bresson's *A Man Escaped*, a German sentinel calls out
to the hero, Fontaine, who has held clandestine meetings: "Always
the same . . . Can't you hold your tongue?" Or literally from the German: Can't you *hold your mouth*? Holding one's mouth, as I have suggested, is certainly a preoccupation of the French cinema, and not
just Bresson's and Tati's. For the French cinema is one of the few
wherein the voice is not self-evident. It's doubtless on account of this
that France has produced some of the most original experimentation
with the filmic voice—Bresson, Tati, Duras, Godard, Straub, and
others—and also the most colorless, drab voices with dull diction.
After Cocteau and Guitry, this cinema continues more than ever to
be a cinema of voices. It is something more and something other
than a "literary" cinema. A cinema of voice-obsessive directors, for
whom saying one word is a dramatic and complicated affair.

FELLINI'S CAULDRON   We need not look far to find the opposite tendency: the Italian cinema, with the vitality and the generous approxima-
tiveness of its post-synchronizing, far removed from any obsessive
fixation with the matching of voices to mouths. The freedom allot-
ted in Italy for the synching of voices is already enormous,[6] but Fellini in particular breaks all records with his voices that hang on the
bodies of actors only in the loosest and freest sense, in space as well
as in time. The French-language version of *Casanova*, supervised by
Patrice Chéreau, is more closely synched than the so-called original
version. It seems Chéreau tried in the French dub to "fix" those huge
disparities between the movement of lips and voices heard, since
French film professionals and audiences alike would tend to cry foul
and complain about the technical errors.

It's interesting to compare the two vocal dubs of the Casanova
character played onscreen by Donald Sutherland. The Italian voice
double, Luigi Proietti, speaks in a rich, throaty voice that lends itself
to sudden bursts and bluster, alternately ingratiating and bombastic.
The French voice double, Michel Piccoli, is precise, ironic, melan-
cholic, lacking in fullness and scope. This voice harks from a school

6. Because of the history of
Cinecittà and its tradition of dubbing voices despite the standardiza-
tion of synch sound elsewhere.

85

where a certain declamatory and rhetorical tradition has been lost. There is anxiety in this voice—the anxiety validated by the entire context of French cinema—of no longer being master of one's voice, of losing one's identity. There is no trace of such an anxiety in the voice assigned to the Italian Casanova. It's not retentive; it's diverse, broad, enveloping—one could even call it communal.

In France the voice is often something people keep to themselves, as if someone might steal it. In Italian cinema, when someone begins to speak, everyone joins in; it's all right to leave behind your own individual vocal contours, then return to them. No one makes a big deal out of it. Fellini takes this convivial side of voices in Italian movies quite far. He plays to the hilt the freedom cinema gives him to mix together voices and accents. At the same time that he succeeds in giving each a very particular silhouette, as Tati does, he also manages to turn them loose together, let them drift and overlap, make voice-balloons in space. He throws them all into a great *cauldron of voices*, shouts, snickers, sighs, and murmurings in various languages. Fellini's movies always leave us with a sense of the jumbled whisperings of a classroom of children, with peals of laughter and the indeterminate sources of voices such that we're often not certain who's talking, X or his deskmate. In Fellini the voice is not something to be mastered or contained, like the Devil. It is mixed and collective, a sort of overall poly-voice each of whose component voices is an individualized emanation. Fellini pokes fun at the notion of being the Master of Voices.

THE CAGED VOICE   It's the same old story: a man wishes to gain control of a female voice, to capture it into the "cage of the screen" as Bazin called it; and also perhaps to capture the intense pleasure this female voice signifies for him—or the elemental power of which this voice is the most archaic sign (for what power could be more elemental for the human being than that of the mother who carried him?). Generally this storyline ends in failure, death, decline, or ridicule. The voice exceeds its confines, eludes the director's will to occupy and control every inch of the screen, and it refuses to be ordered and subdued that way.

TOP: Monsieur Arpel (J-P Zola) and visitors to his factory in *Mon Oncle* (Jaques Tati, 1958).
BOTTOM: Anne Wiazemsky in *Au hasard Balthazar* (Robert Bresson, 1966).

In Fellini's *City of Women*, the famous museum of Dr. Züberkock embodies this grotesque notion of wishing to lord it over female voices and keep them in cages. The collection that the phallocrat has amassed, a *voice museum*, consists of souvenirs of his conquests, in the form of moments recorded and preserved in tape loops. The voices of women with whom he has made love (we can also hear his voice on the tapes) have been recorded during the preliminaries or during sex itself. Accompanying each there is a visual portrait, a large photo transparency of the woman which lights up when you flip a toggle switch. The switch also sets in motion the vocal sequence after a beep, repeating a short loop as long as it's on. Some voices speak ("I want to eat it"), others moan, groan with pleasure, call mama, proclaim their orgasm. Snaporaz (Mastroianni) discovers this museum that occupies a long narrow corridor, and explores it like a kid, turning on voices, his interjections expressing infantile delight. He plays at being the Master of Voices, the master of pleasures, all because he can titillate little buttons and make them cry out.

But while in this place ostensibly made for men's enjoyment Snaporaz finds his own wife in person (Anna Prucnal, who plays a *singer*), she shows him who's really the boss of voices. She pulls a master switch that sets all the voices going at once. Here the screenplay reads: "We hear yet one more woman's voice. But it doesn't issue from the hundreds of tapes, it's not a recording, but the voice of a real live woman at Snaporaz's side. Ironic and hard, it says, "You want to hear them all together, these fine whores?" All the transparencies light up, "loosing their sonic magma"—it's the irrepressible parade of voices and a woman is in command.

In Gordon Willis's *Windows*, a lesbian hopelessly in love with a timid young woman played by Talia Shire tries to appropriate the latter's voice, to steal her cries of pleasure. She pays a young man to go to Shire's apartment and force her at knife point to simulate moans of pleasure. He records the victim's cries and brings them back to the lesbian. Now in possession of Shire's voice, the lesbian listens desirously, endlessly to these extorted sighs, as if she could possess her beloved through her voice. As if that's not enough, she lives in an apartment that faces her victim's across the East River, so she can spy on her with a telescope while simultaneously terrorizing her on the phone. Her victim has a stuttering affliction, known to be a disturbance in the vocal image that returns to the speaker via feedback from her own voice. The scenario of this Bergmanesque little thriller is obviously based on the theme of the mirror and the exchange of identity between a "strong" woman and a "weak" one. Here, as in *Persona*, the voice is a pivot of identification.

As with Elsa in Aldrich's *Legend of Lylah Clare*, by playing too much with the other's voice, the obsessive lesbian lover comes to identify with her. The executioner becomes the victim, eventually vampirized and possessed by the voice she thought herself the master of.

But perhaps the most beautiful story of the man who meets his demise in trying to be the master of voices—to the point of claiming to engender himself through speech—is *Citizen Kane*. The supremely privileged place Welles accords his own voice in his films is well known. He takes pleasure in dubbing secondary characters (e.g. in *Mr Arkadin* and *The Trial*), and in ensuring that his voice is more closely miked than all the others and therefore louder and more convincingly present. Not only does he get the pleasure of playing magician or puppet master, but he can also egotistically claim to be the sole ruler of his own voice.

The extent of this hubris is already established in *Citizen Kane* (hubris: excessive pride which will receive the gods' punishment). *Citizen Kane* is certainly a psychological study and a journalistic tale, but it's as *myth* that I would like to read it now.

KANE: FROM THE WRITTEN TO THE ORAL   The first time Charles Foster Kane is seen in the story of his life, aside from the opening "newsreel" sequence, is on the pages of a book. The reporter Thompson, seeking the key to Kane's dying word "Rosebud," has gone to a library to consult the handwritten memoirs of Thatcher, the man who oversaw Kane's upbringing. The camera "reads" Thatcher's writing, left to right, but when the text is interrupted to go to the next line, the camera continues right and gets lost in the whiteness of the right-hand margin. The blank screen of the white page imperceptibly becomes, through a dissolve, a *page of snow*, a landscape onto which the small form of the young Charlie Kane imprints itself like a letter of type, minuscule in the white expanse.

This is the way the scene begins in which the mother, against young Charlie's wish and despite the lukewarm protestations of an impotent father, signs the contract that will launch the boy into a predestined career. The contract guarantees him the revenues of a gold mine acquired through a fortuitous scrap of paper, which obliges him to embark on a new life with a colossal fortune.

Suffice it to say that doubly trapped—by his mother's unfathomable desires and by the gratuitous and exorbitant gift of this fortune—Kane has his work cut out if he's going to be a "self-made man."

And he certainly does try, by deciding when he reaches majority to liquidate his possessions but not his fortune and to keep only a small newspaper, the *Inquirer*. He works hard to make it a success, and doesn't hesitate to use his money to hire away the competing newspaper's distinguished team of writers. In a word, he *buys pens*. In this way he manages to make the *Inquirer* into an influential paper with a huge circulation.

So at first it's on the basis of *writing* that he tries to build himself up, assuming via the printed word the power to manufacture public opinion and start wars. But this isn't enough for him. He then goes into politics, trying to change the world as an *orator*, rally the people's *voice* (the campaign speech scene). Precisely at this crucial juncture when he's on the verge of success, he chooses to start an adulterous liaison with a young "singer." (These quotation marks are a whole story in themselves. They are seen in the newspaper article that exposes the affair and reduces his political ambition to ashes; and it is in the effort to erase the quotation marks that he'll throw himself into the delusional enterprise of building opera houses and forcing poor Susan to be an

90

opera singer.) He goes up to her apartment where she has invited him. She's an unlikely siren, with her *laugh* and her *toothache*. Once there, he talks to her about his mother; she sings for him, he applauds her.

From then on, everything comes together. His relationship with the quote-singer-unquote is divulged thanks to his political opponent. The people's voice lets him down. Susan's mother had wanted her to be a singer; she fails. Kane wants more and more, and his terrible hunger for power is focused on Susan's voice. He forces her to sing in the opera house he has built for her, where she confronts derisive critics and audience. "We are going to be a great singer," he says to reporters. This "we" bears witness to his amorous appropriation of the other's voice. But since one cannot be the master of another's voice, nor make it an instrument of one's own power when the voice's owner refuses to comply, Kane gets what he was looking for. His reputation is ridiculed, his influence reduced almost to zero.

In other words, with writing, Kane's success had come too easily. He therefore desperately tries to realign himself with the oral, and to forsake, if possible, the advantage of the written. It's as if, long before the contract, the written text that was the foundation of his power, the founding power of a *spoken word*, was lacking for him to establish the very meaning of his existence.

If we see the beginning of *Citizen Kane* as what it is in the film's mythic chronology—a beginning, and not an ending—what do we find? With cavernous, archaic music on the soundtrack, successive landscape shots convey an atmosphere of primal chaos, the primordial jumble in which the elements of land and water are still one. The monkeys as the only traces of animal life hark back to a prehuman past. A light shines in the highest window of a sort of Valhalla. The light goes out and then relights—an effect strongly emphasized by the music. Soon thereafter, the first word of the film issues from a giant mouth, "Rosebud." And the glass ball held by a hand falls and breaks.

We are watching a version of Genesis, in which Rosebud is the first word uttered, whereby there is light. Rosebud is a signifier by

91

definition unanalyzable, since it's the first primordial signifier, pure and simple.

The round ball refers to myths that associate the first manifestation of the Word with a loss of original unity, a fall. In a gnostic myth it is said that during the creation of the world, the *letter* of the Creating Word, its profound essence ascended, while sound "remained below, as if cast out."[7] This myth of the lost original sound is almost universal, even if it's rarely this explicit. It's as widespread as the myth of the fall that occurred when, as sound became language, something had to be lost. There is an aspect here of the imaginary plenitude that was supposedly the total enveloping voice of the Mother in its materiality, where no symbolic dimension has yet come to inscribe the mark of a loss. As Claude Hylblum says, "something of the voice must fall away and be abandoned in order for the child to accede to speech." From this comes the myth of the Golden Age of "full sound," man's dream of a total music-language where the signifier is fully adequate to the signified, without the "chaff" of sound's materiality, where there wouldn't be the dimension of separation and loss; where signification would no longer be born of the *absence* of the thing, but would remain to inhabit the plenitude of the signifier.

So at the beginning of *Citizen Kane* there's an attempt at self-genesis by means of the voice, but a failed one. In testimony to this failure, the light in the window goes out and relights, and finally darkens, like a slow motion, disjointed blink of an eye.

We see this same light in the two opera sequences, where Susan sings her heart out onstage before her voice coach, at the end of his wits, and a terrible and pathetic Kane, his eyes full of mute supplication. At the beginning of the first of these sequences, a fleeting upward camera movement connects the singer's mouth to a closeup of a lamp that goes out.

The second is the montage sequence consisting of images of Susan, in her grotesque operatic poses, with newspaper headlines, long shots of audiences, the voice coach empathetically opening his mouth wide, and the masklike face of Kane fixedly watching her. The sequence is

7. Cited in *La Gnose*, H. Leisegang (Petite Bibliothèque Payot, 1977), pp. 229 ff.

92

obstinately punctuated by flickerings of the diabolical lamp, which finally fizzles out completely, its filament fading into darkness, while the uninterrupted voice, tragic, gamely doing its best, also drops grotesquely in pitch (like the end of Hal in *2001*), precisely accompanying the demise of the light bulb. One couldn't draw a clearer parallel between the demise of the voice and of the light.

Kane's single-mindedness is unable to make him the master of voices, creator of the female voice. Better yet, his effort cannot make him the progenitor of the Word that he was lacking, in establishing him as a subject. The more he tries to be the Pygmalion of a voice (and Professor Higgins was wise to limit his sights to matters of elocution and accent), the more he founders and loses his way.

Rosebud represents lost childhood. But it also represents the fantasy of the primordial word by which the man lacking a father might create himself. But this word arrogantly uttered from the mouth of a would-be God ends up in written form on a sled being thrown into the fire.

Dickie Moore as the young
deaf-mute, and Jane Greer
in *Out of the Past*
(Jacques Tourneur, 1947).

SEVEN THE MUTE CHARACTER'S FINAL WORDS

THE GREAT SECRET* From the very outset there was an essential feature distinguishing the silent movies from canned pantomime. The silent film's characters were not mute, they spoke.

By endowing the film with a synchronized "sound track" and bringing the voice to this added track, the talkies allowed us not only to *hear silence* (until then, on occasions when the continuous musical accompaniment was interrupted, there was no true silence within the fiction itself, but only a silence imposed on the filmgoer by the deaf cinema), but also to have truly silent, mute characters. The deaf cinema, having presented them in among speaking but voiceless characters, wasn't able to *make their silence heard.*

There are more mute characters in the talkies than we might think. How can we possibly consider the talking or sound film without taking them into account? The silent ones of the sound film should bear no particular relation to the silent cinema, and yet . . . In the modern cinema they can represent, by a sort of proxy, the memory of a great Lost Secret the silent movies kept. Is this a simple confusion based on the misunderstood notion of "silent," or does a more meaningful relationship underlie it?

The modern cinema does in fact regard itself as the child of a primitively silent cinema. The period hallowed as the era of its origin is a time we tend to revere as the golden age of the lost secret. "The Great Secret" is also the phrase by which Truffaut named the section of his book *The Films of My Life* which included his writings about the inventors of forms and genres in the era of the "deaf" cinema.

Can we, then, tease the Great Secret out of the silent characters who continue to haunt the sound film? What can they tell us?

HOW MUTE CHARACTERS FUNCTION The question of the functions of mute characters has already been answered to some extent. The mute character serves the narrative, and at the same time often plays a

*This chapter comes from an article of mine entitled "Le Dernier mot du muet," published in *Cahiers du cinéma* no. 330 (Dec. 1981), pp. 4–15 and no. 331 (Jan. 1982), pp. 30–37. For the present volume I have, in the interest of brevity, omitted most of the second half (no. 331), which includes discussions of other well-known mute film characters ranging from Harpo Marx to Elizabeth Vogler in Bergman's *Persona*.

subservient role. Thus he's servant both to a central character and to the fiction. He's rarely the protagonist or the crux of the plot; most often he's a secondary character, marginal and tangential, but also somehow positioned intimately close to the heart of the mystery. Be he there to disturb, catalyze, or reveal, he is most often an *instrument*.

In discussing mute characters it is important to distinguish between *muteness*—a physical condition that prevents the subject from speaking (such as a lesion, or a destroyed nerve center or phonic organ), and *mutism*—the refusal to speak, for so-called psychological reasons, with no physical damage to nerves or organs.

The first question posed by the presence of a mute character in a story is, in fact: is it a case of muteness or mutism? Wherever he turns up, he generates doubt; we rarely know for sure whether he cannot speak or will not speak, and what's more, we don't know how much or how little he knows. His presence also seems to cause any character he interacts with to question their own knowledge, for knowledge is always partial, and the mute might well be the one who knows "the rest."

The mute is considered the guardian of the secret, and we are accustomed to him serving in this way. So the presence of a mute character clues us in to the fact that there is a secret. It may be a nasty sexual secret; recall, for example, the mute male characters of decades past who in the protagonist's shadow suggested the shame of homosexuality. On the other hand it may be a terrifying secret; whatever dangerous game is going on at Count Zaroff's? Or perhaps it is a mythic or cosmogonic secret.

To encounter the mute is to encounter questions of identity, origin, desire. "But who are you? what do you want?" asks Fellini's Snaporaz to the spider-woman in *City of Women*. She fixes her eyes on him and says nothing. Here we find an example of the mute character as a walking reproach. He has merely to appear, and a criminal begins to feel unsure of himself. The mute is often assigned the role of moral conscience, for next to him everyone feels guilty.

Since we cannot easily determine what he knows and does not know, the mute is often assumed to know all, or at least to be keeping to himself the knowledge which in combination with that of the character he is associated with, will resolve the whole intrigue. He is presumed to harbor *the final word*, the key to the quest, but which he cannot or wishes not to utter. We might think of him as the place where the story's crucial knowledge is lodged and which can never be wholly transmitted.

Like many who have been injured or robbed of one of their senses, he may have developed a hypertrophied talent. His eyes are thought to penetrate deeper. He is presumed to see all, as if the deprivation of speech were payment for something he wasn't supposed to have seen. He is sometimes the eye of the fish in Fellini's films, with such a profound gaze that you cannot hide from it. (I'm thinking of the monstrous fish on the beach at the end of *La Dolce Vita*, and of the aristocrat in *Casanova* who watches sex acts through a peephole painted as a fisheye.) In Tourneur's *Out of the Past*, a man who wants to talk privately with Robert Mitchum doesn't know how far away he needs to stand from a deaf-mute boy who can read lips. "Can he read our lips from here?" he asks. "Ask him," replies Mitchum. The mute is the witness, the eyes that were there when it happened.

The mute character occupies an undefined position in space, so that he might emerge from offscreen at any moment. It is as if not being tied down to a voice gives him a sort of angelic—or diabolical—ubiquity. One might find him anywhere without knowing how he got there (the Valet in Black in Losey's 1979 *Don Giovanni*), as if his mutism or muteness extends even to footsteps and other sounds he makes when he moves.

Presumed to have virtually unlimited knowledge and vision, and maybe even unlimited power—in sum, potentially omniscient, panoptic and omnipotent, the limits of his powers never clearly determined—it turns out that the mute, *the body without a voice*, displays many attributes of his counterpart, *the voice without a body*, the acousmatic voice, the voice of one we do not see.

I identify these attributes as "presumed" for good reason. The mute character elicits *doubt* regarding what he knows and can do

97

(and also regarding the knowledge and powers of others), and this factor defines his position in the narrative structure. There is uncertainty about boundaries. Bodies without voices, as well as voices without bodies, similarly seem to have no clear parameters.

Sometimes the mute character is the sage who has seen it all before, sometimes he has made some sort of vow and is going through a process of internal maturation (*Andrei Rublev*, *The Testament of Dr Mabuse*). A famous gag in Dino Risi's 1968 comedy *Kill Me with Kisses* illustrates the passage from imposed muteness to elective mutism. The mute tailor played by Ugo Tognazzi has vowed that if God ever gives him back his speech, he'll join the Trappists.

Finally the mute character may be these things only potentially. The film might be content to present him as a cipher, the servant who brings the coffee or clears the table. But he has only to be called upon, and the most insignificant mute character can be transformed into a disturbingly limitless personage.

As for the mute character and his name, for obvious reasons he does not refer to himself in the first person; he can only respond to the name given to him. Sometimes he doesn't even have a name, which renders him particularly troubling, as if this simple fact gave him the possibility of being everywhere and nowhere at once.

He is most often not the central focus of the story structure, but *near* the center, alongside it—as a double, a conscience, an instrument, a reproach, doubt.

It would be a mistake to think of the mute character as the "opposite" of the character who speaks. The situation is neither one of opposites, nor of reversals, despite what common sense might suggest. If I say that death is the opposite of life, this doesn't get me very far. One might argue that mutism is a corollary and condition of speech, as death is a condition and corollary of life. Beyond that, the mute plays some privileged roles in fiction. First, the role of confederate, double, shadow, and conscience—like the young deaf-mute in *Out of the Past*, or the character played by Krystyna Janda in Wajda's *Without Anesthesia*.

98

Other roles: he might come to embody the death announcement and the debt to be paid. We find this character in Charles Bronson's laconic man of justice in *Once Upon a Time in the West*, and the Black Mask in *Black Orpheus*. Or consider the black-garbed ballerina in Hitchcock's *Torn Curtain*; although not a mute, she never speaks in the scenes with protagonist Paul Newman. These particular examples show the mute character as the executioner. In Littré's dictionary of the French language, one of many definitions of *"muet"* reads: "a person in the service of sultans who, while not prevented from speaking, expresses himself exclusively through sign language. *The sultan sent him mutes, who strangled him."* In this capacity, he can be part of a couple (as in Welles's *The Trial*). But he can fill any other function delegated by an authority or power from above. When mutes are servants, they can also represent the excluded class, those who silently watch the great and the well-to-do embrace passionately and cut one another's throats. As such they take on the sense of a living reproach, and they embody and foreshadow an inevitable final struggle.

On occasion the mute is the object of desire, as long as no one ever succeeds in having her. Think of the adored woman who does not give herself away through words. The young ephebe Giton in Fellini's *Satyricon* remains silent while three men vie for him. With his knowing smile, he seems to be calling the shots. He utters only one word in the whole film. Pronounced in a voice that's obscene in its physicality (a hoarse, vulgar, monstrous voice), the word's purpose is to choose between his two lovers, Encolpius and Ascyltus: "tu," meaning you.

Finally, in that he represents "the rest of the story," the final word, what's left over, the mute character is sometimes there precisely *not to serve*, in order to signify doubt, a void, a lack. The Dogon people of Africa, in their mask rituals, have a deaf-mute mask that is kept physically apart from the others, apparently its only function being to signify nothingness.

All I have said about the function of the mute character in films can apply just as well to mutes in the novel and in theater. Is there anything about the character that is specific to cinema?

The mute in movies raises three major cinematic issues. First, as a body without a voice, he refers back to the origins of cinema, and to the supposed "great secret" of silent film he is presumed to keep.

Second, he refers to everything that early cinema put into play—masking, exclusion, offscreen space. And he elicits the question of all and not-all, of economy and excess in film narrative. By definition the mute problematizes the film narrative's "final word" that supposedly closes off the narrative system as a unified whole.

And third, the cinematic mute brings into play the status of language, speech, and the voice in cinema. A voiceless body, he refers by inference to his counterpart, the bodiless voice of the acousmêtre. The structure of a film like *India Song* consists of the mutual sliding together of an image-track of voiceless bodies, mutes, moving about, and a sound-track where disembodied voices speak among themselves. Which is emphatically not the same thing as slapping a voiceover commentary onto silent images. Duras's film involves the sight of mute bodies and the sound of voices one *could* attribute to them, but always with a slippage, a space between.

FROM VOICELESS BODY TO BODILESS VOICE The cinema maintains a strangely symmetrical relation between the acousmêtre's bodiless voice and the mute character. In both cases, as I have said, the character who has a body but no voice, or a voice but no body, is taken as more or less all-seeing, all-knowing, often even all-powerful. In both cases, the limits of his being and his body generally go undefined (even for the limits of the mute character's body, strange as this may seem), and thus also the limits of his role, his position, his power. And in both cases, unveiling either his voice, or his body and face, has the effect of breaking the spell, re-assigning the character to an ordinary fate, taking away his mythic aura and putative powers. Examples of the mute shedding his silence can be seen in Hitchcock's *Number*

Seventeen, *Persona*, *Satyricon*, and *Elephant Man*. In each case, the unveiling of the voice brings a reversal and the character's "fall" to a common destiny.

We should not belabor the comparison, however, even if the acousmatic character and the mute character meet at two cinematic extremes. One extreme is the image without the voice, a situation created by the silent cinema. The other extreme is the voice without the image, or rather the voice over a dark screen—an extreme often brought into play in experimental films. Of course in many a classical fiction as well, a voice emerges from the dark screen of the credits, or from a dark screen bridging two sequences (Maupassant's narrator in Ophuls' *Le Plaisir*), or even from a formless landscape of peaceful water as in Duras's films or the beginning of Helma Sanders-Brahm's *Germany Pale Mother*. But even though they present obvious symmetries, these two extremes are not interchangeable.

The voiceover and offscreen voice function like a home base, central and autonomous, from which the speaking happens, and it orders, comments, delivers information, and so on. On the other hand, the mute character rarely occupies the center, but almost always is alongside; *someone else* allows him to function by calling upon him. In other words, in order to be a mute in a film, there have to be two of you.

The bodiless voice and the voiceless body can also be, as in *The Testament of Dr. Mabuse*, the two disjointed halves of a single elusive entity. It is readily apparent that this film starts with a voiceless Mabuse, sprung from the limbo of the silent film, and moves toward a bodiless Mabuse. The written part serves as transition, while it also eternalizes the myth. But we cannot say that Mabuse, in acquiring a voice that is always the voice of another, descends to a common destiny. Rather, insofar as he has paid for his mortality with the sacrifice of his mortal body, he is always ready to perpetuate himself. Like Osiris he is always incomplete, each time modeling his being and his power on the media of the time, and especially on the failings of these media, on the unfilled gaps of their representational capacities, and on any kind of "off-screens" that might arise.

THE DEBUREAU EFFECT There's an obvious relationship between mime and mutism, even though the two are by no means the same. Pantomime may be a particular form of speech act. As Frédéric Lemaître says to Baptiste Debureau in *Les Enfants du paradis*, "You speak with your legs, you answer with your hands."

We know that an essential theme of this film is the opposition between pantomime and theater—an opposition that has often served to mark the difference between silent film and sound film, especially at the time when the latter was usurping the former. However Chaplin, who held out against the talking film longer than most, and who defended the silent cinema as an art of "pantomime," knew quite well that the silent cinema was not *only* recorded pantomime, just as the sound film was not only filmed theater. As usual there were few means to conceptualize new genres other than with reference to older genres.

So *Les Enfants du paradis* presents a story in which a mime and a theater actor are in love with the same woman, Garance. As the film opens, she is on display in a fairground stall, nude to the shoulders, as the effigy of Truth. Banal symbolism? And yet this film always communicates an emotional sense that is authentic, universal and, despite its historical setting, less badly dated than the more poetic-realist Carné-Prévert films.

The film was born from an anecdote that Jean-Louis Barrault told to Carné about the mime Debureau (1796–1846). But the story proved not easily adaptable for film without losing its punch. Carné dropped it completely from his scenario, but he retained the character of Debureau; with Prévert he constructed an entirely new story around Debureau, in which the original project resurfaces as an allusion. At the height of his career, Debureau killed a man who was bothering his wife. "There ensued," says Carné, "a trial which *le tout Paris* crowded into, in order to get to hear the voice of the famed Debureau." (We are calling the *Debureau effect* this curiosity about a voice.) But, continued Carné, "if Jean-Louis Barrault acted the part of Debureau as we planned, there would be zero interest in his downfall, since everyone already knew Barrault's voice. If on the other hand we were to cast an unknown actor in the central role, we ran the risk of an indifferent response to the film." These two alternatives obscure the real issue—what precisely do we expect in hearing someone's *voice*, and how can we even imagine for a moment, as did Barrault, Carné, and Prévert, constructing an entire story on a hidden object like this, which cannot even circulate through the narrative, and which once revealed turns out to be no longer desirable? On what, then, is the Debureau effect based? On nothing, we might reply, and that's what makes it unanswerable. This is not a matter of curiosity to know more about someone through what the voice's timbre and intonation reveal. Something else is going on, but what?

We find an example of an effort to use the Debureau effect in *Silent Movie*, Mel Brooks's tribute to silent cinema which itself has sound effects and music but no speech. *Silent Movie* introduces the ultrafamous mime Marcel Marceau for a paradoxical rule-breaking gag. Marceau the mime utters the film's sole word: "No!," to decline an invitation to take part in it. The gag is both ingenious and disappointing, more interesting to talk about than to witness in the movie, better in concept than realization. On the screen we realize how once Marceau's voice is heard, it's "nothing"; the object has been conjured away and can no longer circulate. However, the fact that Mel Brooks made it a mainspring of his film bears witness both to the persistence of the Debureau effect and to the tenacity with which the silent cinema is associated with pantomime.

Les Enfants du paradis refrains from exploiting the Debureau effect proper, but it nonetheless is built on a void. Themes it has aplenty; it even flaunts most of them: art and life, "all the world's a stage," "the show must go on," passion and love, jealousy, class struggle, and the added bonus "there is no sexual relation"—they're all in there, each announced loudly.[1] And it's just that—they are *spoken in the dialogue* instead of coming through in the work, incorporated into the fabric of the fiction; they are not what move the action forward. Paradoxically it is on account of this, in the manner in which the film

1. "There is no sexual relation" is a key formula of Lacan's, meaning roughly that there is no human rapport in the sex act, with respect to the "sexual impasse" which "exudes the fictions that rationalize the impossible within which it originates." Published by Jacques Lacan in *Television* [1974], Denis Hollier, Rosalind Krauss, and Annette Michelson, trans., Joan Copjec, ed. (New York: W. W. Norton, 1990), p. 30. For Lacan, stories in which the lovers are prevented from consummating their desire by some prohibition, belong to this category of fictions.

acknowledges the void over which it is structured, that it is profoundly moving and true.

The action in the film's two temporal settings, teeming with characters and events, revolves around one night of love *which did not take place* between Debureau and Garance, and it resolves around the night of love which does take place between them, in the same room, several years later. Why did it not happen the first time, when Garance offered herself to Baptiste and nothing stood in their way? No reason. Baptiste said, "Oh Garance! Lord knows, I so want you to love me as I love you," after which he simply leaves the room with no warning. We have no idea why, nor does Baptiste, which is what's suggested by the words he uses to impute this non-knowing to Garance. And why does the night of love finally happen years later, by what complex meeting of circumstance and coincidence? There again, there's not much of an answer. It's simply because each decides to be open to it. Once the sexual relationship is consummated, the film has no other course than to end. Garance basically says, "that was wonderful, but I have to leave now," for there has been much water under the bridge. He has married, had a son, and become a famous mime; she has married the count and traveled the world. The film is overwhelming in the way it makes so many years, so many emotions, so many illusions rest on "no reason," a nothingness that illuminates a whole life with eternal regret. But this nothingness, what does it consist of, as an object similar to narrative signs, pieces of cloth, or gold rings, which are the pretext for narrative exchange and circulation through human or cosmic melodramas?

The one who *dis*lodges it in any case, who at some level knows *where it is*, is Garance. Garance catalyzes the action and allows each of the four men who love her to see "his" truth, while she herself exists throughout the film in an irremediable state of existential boredom. All the action takes off from Garance when, in the first minutes of the film, she meets all the men in turn: the sweet talker Frédéric who amuses her, then bores her; then the literary anarchist Lacenaire, who bores her and no longer amuses her, and when she goes to mix in with the crowd during a parade. What captures her attention there is not the "great magical exotic pyrotechnic pantomime" that a barker announces, but what appears to be the spectacle's dregs, a forgotten hanger-on, the expressionless mute with the empty stare, whom the crowd sees as an idiot. It's Baptiste before he has, as it were, spoken for himself. And it is in this moment when the mute has not yet spoken, before he too has begun to utter desiring words to her, to ask her himself for "the last word" which she cannot give, it is in the look of Garance fixed on the empty gaze of the mute who is not yet himself, that she finds this *nothingness* that will circulate and be exchanged, a little of this truth of which others so often make her (with no profit or joy for her) the "guarantor" (which, especially in French, is so close to her name that she is not attached to: "on m'appelle Garance," "they call me Garance").

The Mute Character's Final Words

Thus, this Debureau effect that the filmmakers seemingly evacuated from *Les Enfants du paradis* because it was unadaptable, is precisely what comes into play at the beginning of the film and sets it in motion, serving as an empty, hollow object, like the ring that circulates throughout Wagner's four-opera cycle. The original "theft," if we can put it this way,[2] is when the mute for Garance is still a *place* that she makes into a guardian of something (which she quickly sends back to him, saying to a citizen next to her: "Well, I think he has beautiful eyes"). From then on, everything crystallizes. Baptiste declares himself to be a mime, before the audience and before her (on the occasion of the other theft, Lacenaire's pinching of a bourgeois onlooker's watch). Time passes and does the rest; what results is the mutual love between Garance and Baptiste (impossible love), and also Frédéric's jealousy (which cures him of his endless talking and allows him to become a great actor), as well as the jealousy of Lacenaire (who finally replaces words with action). One only has to see *Les Enfants du paradis* again to understand that this story is patterned with silences that make reference to the mutism and the gaze of the film's beginning. It also provides an explicit reference to an abyss of mutism, innocent in the beginning,

2. That is, comparing Carné's film to Wagner's opera, in which the theft of a ring is the MacGuffin that sets the narrative in motion.

which is what the talking cinema retrospectively constructed as its silent infancy.

The equation of mutism with innocence can be found in the very anecdote that was at the origin of the film. It was because he killed a man that Debureau had to expose his voice to the public. The *nothing-object* that people came to seek in his voice, is located obviously first of all in his mutism (but it is only mutism because it is signified as such by the barker and everyone's gaze), and it is there that it is constituted by the look of Garance as an object (this is what Hitchcock calls the MacGuffin in his own screenplays).

Les Enfants du paradis is thus about a certain impossibility, a certain malediction at work in the relation between language and desire, and wherein the mute plays a role of revealer and of focus of projection. The film refers back to the myth of innocence and knowledge at the time of the silent cinema, the guardian of the "great secret."

Kagawa Kyoko in
Sansho the Bailiff
(Mizoguchi Kenji, 1954).

EIGHT THE SIREN'S SONG

TAMAKI'S LAMENT   Tamaki the mother walks through a forest with her two children, Zushio and his little sister Anju, accompanied by the family maidservant. They are on a journey seeking the father, who has been in exile for having disobeyed his superior, a cruel official who replaced him as Governor. Before taking leave of his family the father had given the boy Zushio the family treasure, a statuette, and had taught him these words: "Be hard on yourself, but merciful to others. Men are created equal, and everyone is entitled to happiness."

The travelers arrive at a lake, and decide to spend the night on the shore. The two children go off to cut reeds and branches for a shelter. Anju tries to break off a tree branch, but it is too strong and she calls Zushio for help. The branch breaks off as both children pull. They fall down to the ground with it, laughing and gay. At this moment, Anju says, "I hear Mother's voice." "It's only the sound of the water," answers Zushio. It turns out indeed to be their mother calling them, worried by their absence.

So the children, and we, hear the mother's voice, apart from her body, like the branch separated from the tree. Zushio takes this plaintive acousmatic voice for the sound of water washing on shore, although we recognize it without difficulty (along with Anju) as a woman's voice. This is not the last time this lingering melodic call will haunt the film. The two children's names, Zushio and Anju, are always heard together, always in that order.

The next day, a terrible scene: the mother and her children are torn from one another at the lake. The mother has mistakenly put her trust in a "priestess" who turns them over to pirates, who in turn sell them into slavery. Tamaki is sent to Sado Island, where she is sold as a courtesan. Anju and Zushio eventually end up working as slaves in the domain of the cruel bailiff Sansho. Anyone who tries to leave Sansho's property will be branded with a red-hot iron.

Years of this painful life go by.

Anju becomes a sweet and submissive girl, now named Shinobu, meaning "to endure." The wound of separation remains forever open in her. Zushio, having lost hope of ever seeing his father or mother, has hardened. He obeys the harsh law of Sansho's domain, and even accepts the chore of branding an old man caught trying to escape.

One day a new slave girl named Kohagi arrives at the Bailiff's domain. Anju sets her up at the loom to work. Kohagi sings a sad song as she toils. We first hear it acousmatically as the camera is on Anju. "How I long for you, Zushio . . . How I long for you, Anju . . ." Anju recognizes her mother's lament transformed into song, a song that has traveled across time and space to reach her through this slave. "Where did you learn that?" asks Anju. "It was a song everyone knew on Sado." "But who sang it?" "A courtesan, I think." Anju weeps.

The song Kohagi sings motivates a scene transition to the coast of Sado Island, where it resonates unrealistically, drowning in echo, as if it were everywhere, a veritable siren song, returning to Tamaki who had originally sent it on its journeys. We then see the mother on the shore, as if she were drawn by this song we hear but which she is not singing, which is detached from her body. She runs down to the beach and desperately tries to persuade two boatmen to take her away from the island. But she is caught and punished; her captors cut one of her tendons so she cannot escape. We see her again on the shore, limping with a cane. In a heart-rending voice she ceaselessly calls Zushio, Anju, always these two names in the same order.

The song carries us once more in space back to the Bailiff's domain, where Anju sings the song over and over. Zushio, exasperated, orders her to stop. He rejects the idea of escape that has rekindled Anju; he thinks they must forget their father and mother and stop being tortured by the hope of ever seeing them again.

One day the two are permitted to go outside the Bailiff's property, in the company of a guard, to carry away an old slave woman to die. They decide to make a shelter for her, so they begin cutting reeds. The scene from childhood returns: brother and sister together in nature, the reed-cutting, the branch they break together with their weight, the same music—and seemingly emerging from everywhere, unreal, the mother's resonant call suspended in the air: "Zushio . . . Anju . . ." Finally Zushio opens his heart, accepts the voice, and weeps. Now he wants to escape. Anju does not go with him. She stays to distract the pursuers, allowing him to flee carrying the old woman. Once he escapes, Anju, who does not wish to be recaptured and tortured into revealing where her brother has gone, takes her own life. She walks slowly into a pond. The mother's song, "Zushio, how I long for you, Anju, how I long for you," more acousmatic than ever, draws her slowly into the water until she is gone; nothing remains but a circular ripple on the surface. Then the song is silent.

Zushio manages to reach the Prime Minister who tells him about his father's death and appoints him Governor.

Zushio's first act as a powerful man is to go and meditate at his father's grave.

His second act is to issue a decree banning slavery. He goes personally to Sansho's domain to have the Bailiff arrested, to find his sister, and to announce to the slaves that they have been freed. He is devastated to learn of Anju's sacrifice.

His third act is to resign from his governorship. A simple traveler once again, he goes to Sado Island to find his mother, whom he has not seen since childhood when he was wrested from her by the pirates. For a moment he thinks he might recognize his mother in an aging prostitute, then loses all hope. But then, he hears an acousmatic song, sung feebly, and its words include his name.

The song leads him to a ramshackle fisher cabin. Behind the hut a blind old woman sings, in a daze, slowly flailing a reed up and down. He falls sobbing at her feet: "Mother, it is I, your son Zushio!" At first, she cannot believe him. He makes her touch the family statue. She recognizes it by feel, she explores her son's face with her fingers, she recognizes him. He tells her of the father's death, then of Anju's. "Only the two of us remain." And as they embrace in tears by the sea, the mother speaks the last words: "If you are here, I know it is because you followed your father's teaching."

This is the simple story told in *Sansho the Bailiff*. No one in the cinema has made the mother's voice resonate like the director Mizoguchi Kenji.

THE MOTHER'S VOICE   Why does the love-filled voice of the mother have this power of death over the girl it draws into the water, while it awakens in the son Zushio a humanity his heart had been closed to for so long?

We mustn't forget that Zushio had received from the father the gift of a wise saying, which the mother recalls to him in the film's last line. The gentle and faithful Anju has never been the beneficiary of such teaching. Between the mother's voice, to which she is totally open, and herself, she has nothing, no direct recourse to the parental word and to Law.

When the acousmatic voice sounds for the first time on the lake shore, Zushio refuses to recognize it; he has made it out as the sound of the water and closed himself off from the voice's power. Anju the girl, who is completely open to it, recognizes it at once. Zushio retains an inner space that he closes off and protects; Anju has nothing like this for herself.

Brother and sister together breaking the branch from a tree, for a mother; proximity to a shore; acousmatic voice of the mother calling their names together—such is the pattern which, repeated years later, will undo the long period of separation, imprisonment, and latency the siblings endure, and which will lead the former to a rebirth and the latter to her sacrifice in death.

In many cultural traditions, trees have a soul that cries out when they are mutilated. Is the mother's voice the voice of the wounded tree? The broken branch evokes the multiple separations that constitute this story: the father from his wife and children, then the children from the mother, then the brother from the sister—until all that remains is mother and son, sobbing in each other's arms.

We can also imagine that this broken branch symbolizes an act of autonomy, and that the mother hastens to reestablish a vocal link with her children who are slipping away from her—a vocal

112

connection to reassert control through her anxiety. Even if her first concern is for Zushio, whom we see in the first shot of the film jumping on a tree trunk across a stream: "Zushio, that's dangerous."

Water is feminine, trees are masculine. Water and the voice are two instances of that which has neither location nor border unless we assign them one. The tree, on the other hand, is a place, and marks a border.

The motif of borders is important in *Sansho the Bailiff*. To move beyond the boundaries of the Bailiff's domain is a crime that will be cruelly punished. Sado island is for the mother a prison that cuts her off from her children. Her cut tendon (the broken tree) imprisons her still more within the bounds of her body, and the lament that originates with her and travels far afield is all the more agonizing.

In this film, water means separation, danger, death. It is the mother's voice that subverts boundaries, that transcends time and space, but for the girl, who can only join her mother in death, in fusion with the water, it is a siren voice that *beckons her to her ruin.*

Sometimes I've asked myself a question that might seem absurd. What would have changed if *Sansho the Bailiff* had been a silent film, obliging us to imagine the mother's voice? What would be different besides, of course, our *really* hearing it (but of what import is this "really")? It seems to me that the answer is this: to the extent that in a silent film the voice wouldn't be materialized, but understood on the basis of images that would signify it, the mother's call would be an image linked to other images, a figure linked to other figures. But the actual voice of Tanaka Kinuyo in fact *comes unglued* from the images, becomes autonomous, lives a life of its own. And we can refuse at first to hear it, as Zushio does, or we can recognize it as Anju does.

The silent film allows us to dream about the mother's voice, as long as the voice is explicitly indicated. The sound film, first making it heard faintly, on the verge of silence, opens up the possibility of *not hearing it consciously* even though it has reached our ears. The most "secret" moment of *Sansho the Bailiff* occurs when the voice resonates for the first time, when it has not yet been named by Anju,

113

nor clearly been identified by a closeup of the mother calling her children, and when the spectator, who has registered it, may still not actively attend to it. When nothing has yet named it, it is a phantom and un-situable object which will continue to wander through the film.

When in the end Zushio reunites with his mother on the shore, guided by her song, Mizoguchi omits the sound of the sea, even though the sea is nearby. It's as if the voice were *in fact* taking the place of the sound of the water that Zushio had made it out to be. There is nothing in common between this sound-film sea that's rendered silent, whose song is replaced by a woman's voice, and the sea of silent films, which appealed automatically to spectators' internal hearing of surf.

The voice and the shore. There is in this film one aspect of the myth of the sirens, and which is rarely mentioned. Sirens are creatures of the *borderline* between land—a solid body, circumscribed—and the sea, which is uncircumscribed, formless. Sirens inhabit the in-between that they invite us to negate, since they invite confusion of land with sea, speech with voice.

SIRENS The voice has to do with boundaries and shores. According to Denis Vasse,

> the fetus, curled up in the mother's womb, feels fluid pressures at the same time as auditory sensations. We now know that the child hears in utero certain frequencies of the maternal voice. . . . As for the coenesthesic sensations caused by the amniotic fluid, they make the body that which resists the invasion of the liquid; they give the body its boundary. It is not by chance that psychotic children's first representations of the body regularly appear on a boat or on a shore—at the boundary of land and water. We can easily see that the first verbal signifiers of the voice become inextricably linked with the coenesthesic sensations of a tension and a boundary that are not yet those of skin, of tactility.[1]

1. Denis Vasse, *L'Ombilic et la voix: deux enfants en analyse*, collection Le Champ Freudien, gen. ed. Jacques Lacan (Paris: Editions du Seuil, 1974), p. 81.

114

Ever since the film screen has been inhabited by the voice that permeates the boundaries of the screen, the myth of the Sirens has haunted it. The silents had more stories about sirens—for example, there's Nina's cry in *Nosferatu* as she calls the vampire to his ruin. But these stories were still written entirely in images, in the totality, the undivided unity that the silent cinema was felt to be. With the sound film, through evolving from suggested sound to actually heard sound, the voice frequently *turns against the image*, seduces it, and unmoors it.

Such a "siren" is heard at the beginning of Godard's *Sauve qui peut (la vie)*. It's the voice of an unseen soprano that sweeps through the bedroom of Jacques Dutronc—a voice summoned or indicated by nothing in the image, but which has its own life. Its aberrant, offscreen presence perturbs the spatial integrity of this hotel room where it doesn't belong; it continues to resonate into the foyer. It is reminiscent of the displaced voices of Marguerite Duras, who is present in this film, too, through her own voice. This ubiquitous female singing voice may be taken as a sort of announcement that the hero will die at the end.

In Lumet's *Fail Safe*, we have last seen the bomber pilot flying toward Moscow to drop his bombs. Once he's reached a critical point in the flight, his formal instructions order him not to turn back for anything, since any voice he hears could well be an enemy diversion. Thus he resists even the entreaties of the president (Henry Fonda). The Americans, having tried everything including missiles to intercept him, deploy their ultimate weapon—a woman's voice. The pilot's wife speaks to him, begs him. And like Ulysses, he has to muster all his forces, fight with his whole body and mind, to resist this beckoning.

A strange film from the early sound era, Lucien Hubbard's *Mysterious Island*, a part-talkie hybrid like *The Jazz Singer*, contains an analogous situation. This time the heroes are in a submarine. By means of an improbable underwater radio apparatus they receive a woman's voice from above, asking them to surface and come to her rescue. We discover later that the voice was a trap. It wasn't Sonia the young heroine calling to them, but a poor woman forced under

TOP: Hanayagi Yoshiaki and Tanaka Kinuyo in *Sansho the Bailiff*. BOTTOM: Lillian Gish and Robert Mitchum in *The Night of the Hunter* (Charles Laughton, 1955).

threat of torture to pretend she was Sonia. At the outset, then, the voice was presented as a vehicle of ruination and entrapment.

TIME SUSPENDED The woman cried out, in the great concert auditorium of Albert Hall, just before the orchestra and choir reached the climax of the "Storm Cloud Cantata." Her shout didn't stop the music, which moved ineluctably on. It simply made the killer's bullet go off course, and saved the life of a foreign prime minister in the balcony.

What did she know of the Albert Hall plot to murder this dignitary she didn't know? Nothing, and yet she guessed it all and screamed, while her husband, the man who knew too much (which is the title of the Hitchcock film I'm discussing—the second version) was unable to warn the police. It is no accident that this woman, Jo Conway (Doris Day), is a singer. Her voice has powers that certainly don't end there.

In fact, soon after the failed assassination attempt, her boy who has been abducted is secretly moved to a room deep inside the very embassy where she happens to be invited to a reception by the man she has saved. She knows her son is hidden somewhere in the place, but where? Impossible to contact the police, for this red-carpeted embassy has immunity—it's impregnable, like a body (in Hitchcock the woman always seems to enter houses where she's not welcome).[2] So, since she can't have the place searched, Jo Conway the singer will use her voice. Before an assemblage who doesn't know what's going on and who urges her to share her vocal talent with them, she chooses to resume the fetish song that she sang to her little boy at the film's outset. "Que sera sera, what will be, will be" is a song whose wisdom is both essential and completely content-free, a song that mothers pass on to their sons, a song that embodies such handing down. As she sings, her voice rises and takes on limitless proportions, amplified by echo. Like the mother's song in *Sansho the Bailiff*, Jo Conway's song takes wing through the empty space of the red-carpeted hallways and stairs; the entire embassy resonates with the song, as a body vibrates from the voice that inhabits it. For a brief while the voice puts off the law and

2. In this Hitchcockian situation the beautiful young woman intrudes on households where there's usually a man living under the influence of a controlling mother figure. The heroine's intrusion—often by surprise—seems often to set the drama and even catastrophe in motion. Think of Ingrid Bergman in Claude Rains' house in *Notorious*, Janet Leigh and later Vera Miles in the old Bates house in *Psycho*, Tippi Hedren in Rod Taylor's house in *The Birds*, and the superb Grace Kelly in *Rear Window*—first in James Stewart's apartment, then in Raymond Burr's.

117

inevitability; bathed in supernatural echo, the voice reaches the little boy sequestered in the far-off room. The kid answers by whistling to the tune. Their connection is established, and by this law-breaking moment that has torn down all barriers, mother and son succeed in finding each other.

We find the voice deferring evil in a similar way but much more movingly, strongly, profoundly, in *The Night of the Hunter*. Marguerite Duras speaks admiringly about this scene in Laughton's film: "[The criminal] sings as before. Before what? Maybe before this beginning of the world heralded by the song. The old woman sings for him. First she sings to make him hear that she is there, to keep him at a distance, that she is awake, watching the children. And then she sings still more. . . . First her song comes across as a challenge, then it is shared by the father, and then, yes, it becomes a song of joy, of celebration. The criminal and the old woman sing together for the return to life, the father's last celebration, and the children bask in this song until morning. They sing their heads off. The song can be heard everywhere. . . . The song becomes the wall that crime cannot scale during the passing of the night."[3]

Here Duras speaks of the effect of suspension or respite, how the voice brings us back to origins, and how it establishes closure at the same time that it goes beyond it.[4]

In the Hitchcock film the scene is much less powerful, for the idea of the protective mother doesn't inspire him as much as the terrifying mother.

John Carpenter's *The Fog*, which I have already mentioned, engages a benevolent mother's voice, which could be a siren voice since it speaks from an abandoned lighthouse. This voice makes connections among various characters who never meet. She has a son, and the father is absent. The separation of the sexes is another of the film's motifs, as in *The Night of the Hunter*.

Out of the sea over which the voice travels a living white fog, which opens out its tentacles to infiltrate the small coastal town. From the top of the lighthouse, the voice-woman (who broadcasts

3. Marguerite Duras, "Les Yeux verts," published as a special issue of *Cahiers du cinéma*, no. 312–313 (June, 1980), p. 62.
4. Denis Vasse says, "The voice creates the boundary that it crosses." See his *L'Ombilic et la voix*, p. 186.

via a radio station) can see this fog, which for those below is indistinction itself, the loss of boundaries. When you're inside it there is no more location, and from this non-place come silent murderous ghosts. The voice-woman is the only being that can identify, locate, and rescue—providing her listeners have adequate reception. Here the voice does battle with formlessness, and with what is formless in it; it confronts the fog as a sort of embodiment of the voice itself.

Only a woman's voice can invade and transcend space like this. No need for a curtain. The curtain drop is a masculine artifice. The masculine acousmêtre must hide for its voice to acquire something of the infinite, and it still occupies a space that can be pinpointed. Even Jehovah, the Great Acousmêtre, occupies a point in space. He can "pass before Moses" at the latter's request, with the interdiction of being looked at.[5] He has a whole apparatus—curtain, smoke, bush—but he occupies a place; it's even to this that he owes his being the Father.

On the other hand, the voice of the woman seems to possess ubiquity by nature.

So everything is different depending on whether it's a man or woman, or a being who is neither one nor the other, having at its disposal this place the screen, on which to speak of love and death with the sea in the background, or to play at the master behind doors or curtains.

THE SCREEN AS A SHORE   "Let the cinema go to hell." These are Marguerite Duras's famous words for the epigraph of Le Camion. The phrase caused quite a stir in France, and reverberated through the filmmaking profession itself. Then when Duras published an essay in Le Monde asking everyone who knew they'd detest L'Homme Atlantique not to go see it, all hell broke loose. The editorial writer of a French film magazine felt obliged to show the blow had struck home by publishing a long essay that might serve as an antidote to Duras's perceived "elitism" and the effects it might have on the moviegoing

5. See Exodus 33.

119

public. As if Duras' voice, which speaks only in her name, had the power to put a curse on the entire film industry!

The idea that the voice is the tool of cinema's ruin has already been uttered, but that was more than sixty years ago, at the beginning of the talkies. And people didn't even use the word voice; they said "sound," "talkies," and "dialogue." But as I've already said, what else besides the voice (and not dialogue, which already existed in silents) could destabilize and compromise the cinema? What did the cinema have to lose? "Innocence"—which was attributed to it only in retrospect, once it had acquired voices? Several months before, no one knew that the cinema was in its golden age of innocence, or even that it was "silent."

The cinema's perdition, the cinema's loss: this can mean to get lost as in a desert, or as in the contourless ocean. Marguerite Duras's films often include the sea, in image or sound, the ocean seen or heard from the shore. The screen in her films is often like an edge, a shore, inhabited by acousmatic voices, siren voices calling the cinema to its ruin. Isn't it from the shore that the image of the sea communicates the strongest feeling of boundlessness? And isn't the screen, the frame, often a shore?

One film by Duras in particular, *L'Homme Atlantique*, gives the impression of being on a shore of cinema before the sea. Beneath the author's voice we hear (or think we hear) the sound of waves, so faintly that it might just be minute bits of background noise on the soundtrack—unless it's precisely this background noise, this contourless white noise, that may be mistaken for the sound of the sea.

This film is famous for essentially consisting of what one expected to see Marguerite Duras doing one day: an acousmatic voice speaking over a dark screen. If she isn't the first and only one to have done it (for it appears temporarily in numerous films, like at the beginning of *M*), no one else has used it in quite this way. First, *L'Homme Atlantique* isn't a black screen from beginning to end. The screen occasionally lightens to show the seaside seen from a window, and a man, silent, in a hotel.

120

A dark movie theater, the voice of a woman and, now and then, images: is that all there is to *L'Homme Atlantique*? No, for when the screen is dark, *it doesn't mean there is no longer a place*. The frame, the space of the projection, even when dark, continues to exist and remains visible. If the images we see were those of a film that stops now and then, everything would be different. It's the obvious frame, this black window created by the projection of the black filmstrip, that makes it so there's still a film. And it's with relation to this fixed, framed place that the voice can play in the dimension of boundlessness, no-place, perdition. *Because there is a place*, and because this place is that of *not seeing everything*. It is thus that we can best define, after Bazin, the film screen.

It seems that in the cinema it is the screen, this place of not-seeing all, that confers on the voice its effects of mystery, power, and transcendence, and even a supposed all-seeing quality. The screen lets

it play with the lure of a power that might be taken back at any time—precisely, through making things visible. For example, it can turn the limitation of not-seeing-all (at once) into the challenge of showing-all (gradually).

For showing everything, including the unshowable region of off-screen space, think of pornography and violence, which leave nothing to the imagination. They leave nothing to say either. These are images to render the voice speechless. To which there is a symmetric response, the renunciation of showing anything in *L'Homme Atlantique*, and its voice with its infinite echo.

The idea of a voice that leads the cinema to its ruination is a compelling one, but one that isn't true. It is simply not the case that the cinema is "dead." The cinema of perdition is not the perdition of cinema—to the contrary. Isn't it to movie theaters that we love to come to lose ourselves? The voice, in this invitation to perdition, is perhaps the most seductive of ushers.

III. NORMAN; OR, THE IMPOSSIBLE ANACOUSMÊTRE

Preben Lerdoff Rye and
Ann Elisabeth in *Ordet* (Carl
Theodor Dreyer, 1954).

NINE THE VOICE THAT SEEKS A BODY

SCARS AND SUTURES Contemporary Western culture resolutely claims to be monistic, fiercely rejecting the dualistic idea of man split down the middle. The liberal, "emancipated" ideal becomes to reconcile the fragments of the self all within the body, considered as the homogeneous and unsplit habitat of the individual.

The sound film, for its part, is dualistic. Its dualism is hidden or disavowed to varying extents; sometimes cinema's split is even on display. The physical nature of film necessarily makes an incision or cut between the body and the voice. Then the cinema does its best to restitch the two together at the seam.

(Let's remark in passing that the notion of the voice as a separate and autonomous entity didn't arise with the invention of the gramophone and the telephone, devices that separate the voice from its source in the body. The idea of recording the voice is documented in ancient myths—Midas and Echo, for example—as well as in Rabelais's famous "Frozen Words").[1]

But isn't the talking picture precisely a form that reunites and reassembles, more than it cuts in two? If we're talking about cutting voice from body, shouldn't this apply more to radio or telephone than to cinema?

The answer is no. Neither radio nor telephone, nor their complement, the silent cinema, is dualistic. Isolating the voice as they do, telephone and radio posit the voice as *representative* of the whole person. And a character in a silent film, with her animated body and moving lips, appears as the part of the whole that is a speaking body, and leaves each viewer to imagine her voice. So in explicitly depriving us of one element, both radio and silent cinema cause us to dream of the harmony of the whole.

If the talking cinema has shown anything by restoring voices to bodies, it's precisely that it doesn't hang together; it's decidedly not a seamless match. Garbo's voice inspired prodigious amounts of

1. [In an oft-cited episode of the adventures of Pantagruel, the heroes traveling by boat in the northern seas hear shouts and noises of war. They figure out that these are the sounds of a battle that took place there months before during the cold season, and that the cold had frozen the sounds. The thaw has released them into the air. See *Le Quart Livre des faicts et dicts héroïques du bon Pantagruel*, 1548, chapters 60 and 61. *Trans.*]

commentary when it was finally heard in *Anna Christie*. From the finely chiseled beauty of her facial features no one could have imagined her voice would be so husky. Some critics even tried to attribute it to microphone distortion. But other stars also paid dearly when their own real voices were judged shrill and badly matched to their physiques, or, if you will, badly matched to the body-cum-voice that their silent films had let viewers dream about.

Indulging in a bit of ontogenesis, let us revisit the formation of the human subject. We are often given to believe, implicitly or explicitly, that the body and voice cohere in some self-evident, natural way, that becoming human consists for the child of "coming to consciousness," and that's just how it is. All the child has to do is put together the elements given to him separately and out of order. The voice, smell, and sight of "the other": the idea is firmly established that all these form a whole, that the child needs only to reconstitute it by calling on his "reality principle." But in truth, what we have here is an entirely *structural operation* (related to the structuring of the subject in language) of grafting the non-localized voice onto a particular body that is assigned symbolically to the voice as its source. This operation leaves a scar, and the talking film marks the place of that scar, since by presenting itself as a reconstituted totality, it places all the greater emphasis on the original non-coincidence. Of course, via the operation called synchronization, cinema seeks to reunify the body and voice that have been dissociated by their inscription onto separate surfaces (the celluloid image and the soundtrack). But the more you think about synchronization, the more aware you can become, as Marguerite Duras did, of the arbitrariness of this convention, which tries to present as a unity something that from the outset *doesn't stick together*.

This does not mean we should scorn those who seek an absolute co-incidence, who attempt scrupulously to reestablish the truth of original sound on original images, to recreate a totality. Such a quest partakes in those wild dreams of unity and absolutes that motivate people to tread the paths of creativity.

It's clear that if voice and body do not hang together in the sound film, the problem does not lie in some technical lacuna. Adding relief, smell, or touch wouldn't change anything, nor would higher-fidelity recordings or a more scrupulous localization of sound. It is as an inherent consequence of the material organization of cinema that the voice and body are at odds.

So back to our ontogenetic subject: at some point, the voice of the other as well as his own voice, gets anchored *somewhere* and doesn't move much from there. If there is a *somewhere* of the voice, a place that is the place of vocal production, is the cinema capable of filming it?

PLACING THE VOICE'S SOURCE At what point should it be said that someone's voice in a film is "offscreen"? The answer is, when it can't strictly be localized to the symbolic place of vocal production, which is the mouth; the answer is, when the mouth isn't visible.

I say symbolic, because otherwise vocal production—phonation—involves many other parts of the body: the lungs, muscles involved in breathing, the larynx, the brain, and so on. So it paradoxically appears that the human body does not have a specific organ for phonation in the way that the larynx is an organ for the regulation of breathing, for example.

If an actor's mouth isn't visible onscreen, we cannot verify the temporal co-incidence of its movements with the sounds we hear. Such audio-visual matching is the ultimate criterion for attributing the voice to a given character. We all know how crucial this factor is for the movies; dubbing is predicated on it in order to fool us. It functions not so much to guarantee truth, but rather to authorize belief.

The mouth may well be the first part of the human body that the movies ever shot in closeup. In a 1901 short by the British photographer James A. Williamson, *A Big Swallow*, the person who is the "big swallower" approaches the camera threateningly. His mouth opens as wide as a house to swallow up the camera, the cameraman, the image (which goes totally dark) and in a way, the spectator too. It's as if one

127

of the first challenges for the movies was to film this black hole, this dispenser of life, this cavity that threatens to devour everything.

The silent film spectator hung on every word from the lips of the star, even if she didn't really hear the voice that came from them. The origin of this oral fixation—for that's what it is—is no doubt the child's early relation to the mother's mouth. It is through the mouth that the child receives everything, eats, cries, vomits, and where it experiences some of its first identifiable bodily sensations.

The singing mouth was one of the first great subjects of the cinema. Filmed opera, with or without the sound of the voice, was one of the first film genres. But singing is one particular mode of vocal production. For singing, the entire body mobilizes around the voice and the modulating air column that emerges through the open lips. So here the outpouring voice is filmed for itself. On the other hand the spoken utterance, which conveys words, emotions, or a message, makes all the more apparent the *cinema's diversion of attention from the "whole" human being to just its voice*,[2] the absence of the body from what the mouth is saying, the voice's very denial of the body.

One could reasonably contest the idea that the mouth is the sole place to film as the source of vocal production. If filmmakers are attached to the mouth for filming the voice, this is also because it affords the most precise cues for synchronization.

SYNCHRONOUS MAN   When you think about it, synchronism, this factor we hold to be so important for knitting the voice to the body, is a strange thing indeed. The word involves the dimension of time (it consists of the Greek roots for "together" and "time"). It allows us by reading a speaker's lips to verify whether the articulation of the words heard accords with the movement of the mouth. These movements are all that can be seen of vocal production, the rest being internal (glottis, vocal cords, lungs) or invisible (air column). We take this temporal co-incidence of words and lips as a sort of guarantee that we're in the real world, where hearing a sound usually coincides with seeing

2. But not in Straub and Huillet's films, with their unique way of centering the actor's body around diction, and their insistence on direct sound.

its source—with allowances for distance (e.g., thunder is not synchronous with lightning, because light travels faster than sound).

So synchronism stresses the temporal dimension, for it seems that the *spatial* factors in voice and image are too uncertain. In fact the greatest arbitrariness does prevail with regard to space. The proof is that today's stereo sound can be played with complete spatial incoherence between what we see and what we hear, without bothering much of anyone except specialists. We rarely find in a film a closeup character and his voice far away (even though it's a lovely effect). On the other hand, we tolerate the opposite arrangement quite easily—characters in long shot with closely miked voices—in fact we welcome it, and it's just as unrealistic.

The prevailing conventions that allow the spectator to assume a voice belongs to a given body onscreen are thus quite variable. We don't need constantly to confirm this co-incidence visually, but it is important that now and then we can recognize the coded signs that guarantee it for us. If the person who's speaking suddenly turns away from us, we're not going to panic because we can't verify the synchronism; we take it on faith that the voice we continue to hear continues to belong to the character. The process of "embodying" a voice is not a mechanistic operation, but a symbolic one.[3] We play along in recognizing a voice that comes from an actor's body as *his*, even if we know the film is dubbed, provided that the rules of a sort of contract of belief are respected, much as with the tacit rules of editing that Bazin explored.

Much Italian cinema, and Fellini in particular, synchronizes voices to body more loosely. In Fellinian extremes, when all those post-synched voices float around bodies, we reach a point where voices—even if we continue to attribute them to the bodies they're assigned—begin to acquire a sort of autonomy, in a baroque and decentered profusion. On the other hand, there are films in which voices are synchronized precisely, screwed tight onto their bodies. Then you get *synchronous man*, direct and human. At the end of Dreyer's *Ordet*, the madman Johannes pronounces before the body of Inger the words that are

3. [Chion's term translated here as "embodying" is *mise-en-corps*, putting-into-a-body, the spectator's attachment of a voice to a body. *Trans.*]

129

supposed to bring the young woman back to life. Dreyer could have filmed this scene in either of two ways. He could have shown the face of Inger when the offscreen words of Johannes are heard, or the camera could remain on Johannes as the latter declaims the words of life.

The first solution would be more magical—Johannes's voice would function as an acousmatic voice with all the power of acousmêtres. The second solution keeps things in the human dimension—Johannes is nothing but a man, and the words have no power other than by the grace of God. This is the solution Dreyer chose. In the entire film, vocal production is filmed directly, head-on, with very few offscreen voices. Speech draws on the symbolic force of "embodied" language here, not on the black magic of disembodied voices.

There is in *Ordet*, however, one moment that does feature an acousmatic voice. This moment does not involve Johannes (who is only a man), but Inger, the young mother, before her ill-fated birth pains. We see her in the house quietly humming to herself. Her contented humming continues over an unexpected cut that carries us outdoors into the countryside where we see for a brief moment one of the men walking. And it's as if, just for an instant, the whole outside world were placed under the protective wing of her voice. Such is the sole moment in *Ordet* of acousmatic, gentle magic.

NAILING AND RIGGING   Marguerite Duras coined the idea that the contemporary cinema stringently requires voices to be *nailed down* to bodies. It's this nailing, which is for her a form of cheating, that she tried to break with in *India Song*.[4] Here she unfastened the voices and allowed them to roam free. "Nailing-down" nicely captures the rigidity and constraint in the conventions that have evolved for making film voices appear to come from bodies.

What we might call an *ideology* of nailing-down is found for example in the French and American film traditions. More than others, these cinemas seem obsessively concerned with synchronization that has no detectable "seams."

So this nailing-down via rigorous post-synching: is it not there to

4. [Duras' and Chion's term is
"vissage," literally screwing-down
or screwing-in. *Trans.*]

130

mask the fact that whatever lengths we go to, restoring voices to bodies is always *jerry-rigging* to one extent or another? As is, ultimately, this localization of voices onto bodies that we learn to do, starting with the voice of the mother.

Several of the very first spectators of talkies were aware of this effect. Alexandre Arnoux, for example, went to London to gather first impressions of the new sound movies and wrote for French readers:

> Right at the start the general effect is rather disconcerting. Since the loudspeaker installed behind the screen never changes its locus of sound propagation, the voice always comes from the same spot no matter which character is speaking. The synchronization is perfect, of course, but it confuses and annoys the listener. If this annoyance is analyzed, it is soon seen that by the very fact that it has been achieved, the concordance of lip movements and spoken syllables strengthens our demands for credibility and forces us to locate the sound in space—in fact, makes this absolutely indispensable. Otherwise, we are faced with a strange comedy in which the actors are closely miming the lines with their mouths, while a mysterious ventriloquistic chorus leader, rigid and motionless [behind] the center of the screen . . . takes charge of the audible part of their silent speeches.[5]

What would Arnoux have said about everything that's permitted today, all the novel techniques orienting sound in space less realistically than ever? But we now know how the sound film developed—along the lines of establishing tolerances, approximations.

Finally, why should we care at all about jerry-rigging, nailing-down, dubbing, synch sound, playback, or ventriloquism? Well, sometimes it matters and sometimes not. In the burlesque strain of film comedy—e.g., Chaplin, Laurel and Hardy, and the Marx Brothers—when we call it jerry-rigged, nothing ontological is at stake. These films often play on the very situation of the human being as a dislocated body, a puppet, a burlesque assemblage of body and voice. If we stop believing for

5. In *Pour Vous*, 1929; quoted by René Clair in *Cinema Yesterday and Today*, R. C. Dale, ed., Stanley Appelbaum, trans. (New York: Dover, 1972 [1970]), p. 128.

a moment in the unity of the body with the voice, it is "serious" dramatic movies whose effect is more readily threatened.

Ordinarily, the goal of dubbing is to outfit a body with an "appropriate" voice. Another use of dubbing occurs more rarely, for it produces a profound malaise: constructing a monster with a completely inappropriate voice (in terms of sex, age, facial features, or expression). This idea has been tried mostly in horror films, giving a hoarse and vulgar voice for example to the little girl in *The Exorcist*. Among monsters created this way we can also cite Giton in Fellini's *Satyricon*, that silent ephebe who pronounces only a single word in the entire movie, in a low, obscene voice; or similarly, the masked bellboys in *Lola Montes*, with their bestial voices. Comedy also has occasionally found amusement in exchanging male and female voices. In *Singin' in the Rain*, there's the famous sequence during a screening of an early talkie getting calamitously out of synch. But in general, filmmakers avoid prolonging this effect since the laughter it produces subsides quickly.

So we easily accept the dubbing of a voice onto a body as long as realist conventions of verisimilitude regarding gender and age are respected (a woman's voice goes with a shot of a woman, an old man's voice with an old man's body). On the other hand, spectators don't easily tolerate a voice dub of the opposite sex or markedly different age onto the body represented onscreen.

THE VOICE OF ANOTHER The idea of dubbing was born with the sound film itself. When Hitchcock made his first talkie *Blackmail* in 1929, it had been conceived as a silent film. He decided to adapt it for sound by shooting several additional scenes. His main actress, Anny Ondra, was German and spoke English badly. So he had her "dubbed," while shooting, by "an English actress, Joan Barry, who did the dialogue standing outside the frame with her own microphone, while Miss Ondra pantomimed the words."[6] He directed Anny Ondra while listening to Joan Barry through headphones. Hitchcock's inventiveness is well known, yet he wasn't alone at the time in employing this

6. F. Truffaut, Collab., Helen G. Scott, *Hitchcock* (New York: Simon and Schuster, 1967), pp. 46–47.

technique of using the *voice of another* on the set.

The voice of another, of a double, is the theme of *Singin' in the Rain* (1952). The story is well known: Gene Kelly and Jean Hagen are a famous star couple of silent movies; then along comes sound. Oops—Jean Hagen has a shrill, nasal, piercing voice. What to do? Donald O'Connor finds the solution. Without the audience knowing it, Jean Hagen will be provided by the charming voice of Debbie Reynolds, Gene's girlfriend. The film makes a big splash at the gala premiere, the audience shouts for Jean and demands to hear her sing onstage in the flesh. To save her, Debbie Reynolds is asked to be Jean's live voice-double, hiding behind the stage curtain while the actress mouths the song. But Gene, Donald, and the producer get a sudden inspiration. They raise the curtain and unveil to the audience Debbie singing behind Jean. An astonishing shot reveals the two women, one behind the other, with the two microphones lined up, both singing with this single voice that wanders between them looking for its source. The audience understands and attributes the voice to its true body. Jean Hagen slips out, and Gene Kelly wins the audience's affection for Debbie. The voice carries the day in this strange contest where men, those who decide whether to raise or lower the Mabusian curtain, play at being masters of the voice.

This plot did not spring fully clothed from the imagination of writers Betty Comden and Adolph Green. From the very beginning, the sound film introduced the possibility of lending someone the *voice of another*.

This situation in which *one woman's voice passes for that of another* is also found in other sound films such as Bergman's *Persona*, and Aldrich's *Whatever Happened to Baby Jane* and *The Legend of Lylah Clare* (which I will discuss further on).

One man's voice passing for that of another is the crux of the plot of Lang's *Testament of Dr. Mabuse*. In fact, we might consider this situation dictated in its dramatic workings by the very principle of the sound film.

Oskar Beregi and Rudolf
Klein-Rogge (superimposed)
in *The Testament of
Dr. Mabuse.*

Thus, no sooner was the sound film born than it showed the human voice in the dimension of doubt and deception, but also of *possession*.

THE VOICE SUPPLANTS THE SUPERIMPOSITION Few dramatic genres are as prone as the sound film to lend the voice the roles of soul, shadow, and double; this occurs because of the invention of the filmic acousmêtre.

The silent cinema was rich in stories of ghosts and doubles, yet it did not have the resource of the voice. Unable to use the acousmêtre, it used a device which the voice would supplant with the coming of sound—the *superimposition*.

The silent cinema relied on superimpositions for three specific purposes. First, you could signify a sound heard by characters (clock striking, musical instrument, train whistle, knock at the door) by showing the image of the sound's source at the same time as the image of the character hearing it. This device indicated the sound's simultaneity, whereas indicating a sound through cutting would suggest that the imagined sound was intermittent. Second, superimpositions were used to show apparitions, doubles, or ghosts. Third, they were employed to signify a character's thoughts or subjective perceptions.

As I have suggested, these three functions of the superimposition, among others, were rapidly superseded in the sound film by acousmatic sound. (For practitioners of the time, sound was already in itself a sort of parallel dimension or superimposition.) In a number of films one finds the two devices coexisting, one visual and the other auditory, as if mutually reinforcing one another.

In fact, sound supplanted the superimposition
- (of course) to signify sounds,
- also in order to embody doubles and ghosts,
- and finally, to signify thoughts, imaginings, and subjective perceptions (for example the scene of Marion's "voices" as she drives in *Psycho*).

The Testament of Dr. Mabuse, a transitional film bringing a silent movie protagonist to the sound screen, executes a kind of handover or transfer of power from the superimposition to the acousmatic voice. It does so by virtue of using them in combination. Lotte Eisner confirmed this revelation: "Lang tells me that these days he would not use the device of the superimposed apparitions of Mabuse's ghost, which he judges clumsy; he prefers a "voice-off" to guide the doctor's crazy careering, which ends . . . in front of the gates of the asylum."[7] But he still used the superimposition, as if seeking to reinforce the experimental new device of the acousmatic voice with the silent convention. In certain scenes, the visual superimposition of a phantom appears to duplicate and reinforce the "vocal superimposition" of Mabuse's voice. The same is true of the shadow outlined behind the curtain, which appears during flashes of light, acting as a double and guarantee, in a sense, of the Master's voice.

The Voice That Seeks a Body

One might see this as a sign of weakness or lack of confidence. Yes, but The Testament of Dr. Mabuse is also about this passing of the torch from silent to sound, from the disappearing superimposition to the acousmatic voice, which would gradually win over the cinema—indeed, sometimes to the point of engulfing it (Duras). This is entirely evident in the scene where Baum is hypnotized by Mabuse's ghost.

Alone in his office, Baum is reading the manuscript of his patient, the Testament written in a trance by the mad scholar, collected and put in order by the asylum staff. "Herrschaft des Verbrechens," the Empire of Crime, is the title of this text that's at first disjointed and frenzied, then organized. Coming as it does in 1932, it of course pointedly suggests a denunciation of Nazism on the rise, since it is presented as a method of gaining power through the terror generated by inexplicable actions.

So Baum is reading this will aloud to himself. For his own voice the film then substitutes *another*, that of an acousmêtre, which takes over: a closeup voice, the insinuating whisper of the hypnotist. It seems at first to be a so-called subjective voice; Baum's lips remain closed, and his eyes are lowered onto the manuscript. Then he sud-

7. Lotte H. Eisner, *The Haunted Screen* [1952], Roger Greaves, trans. (Berkeley: University of California Press, 1973), p. 325.

denly raises his eyes; across from him, the ghost of Mabuse in super-imposition is speaking to him, in an increasingly demented way.

Fascinated by the apparition, Baum remains still. The superimposition compounds itself: a double rises out of the seated ghost. Across from this standing Mabuse, there appears next to Baum in the mirror yet a third Mabuse. While Baum is under the spell of the first ghost seated before him, the third turns the pages of the Testament, and *enters Baum*. Then, with a sound of kettledrums, the three ghosts fade away at once. A high continuous sound is heard during the scene, with a sudden accent just before Baum raises his eyes. The scene is brief, rigorous, terrifying.

What has happened? The silent Mabuse produced a written text, which had been waiting for someone to decode. And when Baum looks at it, *through reading it out loud he unleashes its force*. In turn this reading voice summons *another voice*, an I-voice that inhabits him and then becomes the voice of a ghost that becomes visible, immobilizing him with hypnotic eyes.

This is an example of possession by the "Stimme" (voice), against which one is powerless, what the Peter Lorre character evoked with such terror in Lang's earlier film *M*. So from the text to the voice, and from the voice to the look, Mabuse works his way to ever greater power. During the silent era, he was a hypnotist and acted through the look. *The Testament* refers to that only in brief moments of close-ups on blankly staring eyes. But on the other hand, the film deploys the new power exercised *by texts* and above all *by the voice*—just as there is a succession from the visual device of superimpositions to the auditory device of the acousmatic voice.

As for the voice of this ghost, it is of capital importance, since it's the only moment in the film where we have a voice on a body of Mabuse. But the body is transparent and monstrous, and the voice is unreal. Neither its age nor its sex is certain, perhaps like the voice of the original phallic mother, or the combined voices of the father and the mother in the primal scene. Such a voice often goes with someone who is possessed: too low and harsh for a woman, too high for a man.

138

The theme of being possessed by a voice figures also in Robert Aldrich's *Legend of Lylah Clare*. Lylah Clare is a deceased movie star who has become a legend. Her Pygmalion, who as we'll learn is also responsible for her death, is the director Zarkan (Peter Finch). The latter is looking for an actress to fill the role onscreen in a biographical movie about the star. He is going to repeat with the new woman the story that led the first to her death. A nice young woman named Elsa (Kim Novak) is chosen to play Lylah, and she is asked to let her character penetrate into her. She becomes Zarkan's mistress. We know we've seen this story before. . . .

Elsa achieves perfect identification with Lylah the day she fuses with the dead woman *through her voice*. A cinematic simulacrum fittingly becomes the means and the place of this fusion.

A scene of one of Lylah's films is shown on a projector to Zarkan, Elsa and others. Elsa, who knows the scene by heart, begins to utter the lines of the dead woman who speaks on screen. The projectionist, who gets what's happening, lowers the volume of the film soundtrack. Now there are no longer two simultaneous voices but only the image of Lylah that continues silently while the living Elsa dubs her live, giving her a voice that's *exactly like the original*. Zarkan and the others are transfixed; they're seeing Lylah come back to life. From this day on, Elsa is possessed by Lylah Clare.

Dubbing normally consists in replacing an onscreen character's voice with the voice of another. Diabolically here, the situation is reversed. By imitating Lylah's voice, Elsa is dubbed, so to speak, by the dead woman. But you do not lend your living voice *casually* to the recorded body of a dead person. Elsa will relive Lylah's fate, and she will die her same death.

In her trances when possessed, she has a harsh and obscene voice, its sex and age indeterminate, and she has a demonic laugh, which makes you think it can't possibly be she. It reminds one of moments when a child doesn't recognize its mother; she cannot be this person where violence or sexuality reside, she must be someone else.

139

IMPOSSIBLE EMBODIMENT   So Elsa succeeds only too well in doubling Lylah Clare, that is, in having herself dubbed by her, because she has been imprudent enough to make her voice resemble the dead woman's voice.

Psycho explores a parallel situation of an impossible attachment of a voice to a body, or what I am calling impossible embodiment.

In French, the term *embodiment* (mise-en-corps) is reminiscent of *entombment* (mise en bière) and also to *interment* (mise en terre). And we are, in effect, dealing with something related to a burial.

Burial is of course a symbolic act; some say that it was even the first symbolic act distinguishing human beings from the other species. To bury someone is not merely to dispose of the body for purposes of hygiene. It also means designating a place for the soul, the double. Or for those not believing in an afterlife, it is a place for what remains of the person *within us* or for us. Burial is marked by rituals and signs such as the gravestone, the cross, and the epitaph, which say to the departed, "You must stay here," so that he won't haunt the living as a soul in torment. In some traditions, ghosts are those who are unburied or improperly buried. Precisely the same applies to the acousmêtre, when we speak of a yet-unseen voice, one that can neither enter the image to attach itself to a visible body, nor occupy the removed position of the image presenter. The voice is condemned to wander the surface. This is what *Psycho* is all about.

Much has been written about *Psycho*. Most analyses neglect to consider the role of the *mother's voice* as an acousmêtre. The mother in *Psycho* is first and foremost a voice. We catch occasional glimpses of some mute, bestial monster waving a knife, or a shadowy figure behind the window curtains of her room (like Mabuse's shadow behind the curtain). And fleetingly also on the landing of Norman's and his mother's house, we glimpse a body carried by Norman. But the voice—cruel, insistent, and certainly not fleeting—is always heard at length offscreen.

The three speeches delivered by the mother's voice are heard at three turning points in the plot. The first occurs when Marion, freshly arrived at the motel, overhears the argument between Norman and his mother. Second, there is the scene on the landing, when we hear offscreen another equally stormy discussion between Norman and his mother; he's trying to take her down to the basement. It ends with an apparent de-acousmatization. The third occasion closes the film: Norman is shown in his cell, completely possessed by his mother.

1. *The argument.* Norman (Anthony Perkins) is the young man who manages the motel where Marion (Janet Leigh) ends up after her escape from Phoenix. He proposes that Marion come up and have some dinner in the old house that he shares with his mother next to the motel. While he goes up to the house, Marion settles into her motel room. That's when she overhears a row offscreen, coming from the house, between Norman and an old woman with a hard, powerful voice that also sounds far-off and improbably bathed in reverb. The "acousmother" unleashes her anger at her son's gall, this libidinous boy, in proposing to bring a strange woman into *her* house. Norman returns to the motel shortly thereafter and apologizes. He explains that "Mother isn't quite herself today," and that he has to take care of her all by himself.

The obvious function of this scene is to set the acousmatic mechanism in motion. In other words, even before the murder, it *creates the desire to see what is going on.* In fact, it is the law of every offscreen voice to create this desire to go and see who's speaking, even if it's the most minor character (provided that the voice has the potential to be included into the image; it can't be the disengaged voice of commentary).

From this point forward, the story is propelled by the obsessive idea of getting into the house in order to see the mother. The violation of the family home by a woman is, as we know, a typically Hitchcockian scene and generally has dramatic consequences. *Rebecca, Notorious, Rear Window, The Man Who Knew Too Much* (1956), and *The Birds* all provide examples. But here, entering the house equals finding the source of the voice, bringing the mother onscreen, attaching the voice to a body. Soon after the first occurrence of the

Anthony Perkins
in *Psycho.*

acousmêtre, a tall, mute and savage creature, whose physical details we do not see and who we are led to believe is the mother, suddenly appears and stabs Marion to death in her shower. We will see the same ambiguous figure later, going out onto the second-floor landing in the house, to exterminate the detective Arbogast in much the same way.

Here it could be said, "So you've got your embodiment already—there's your acousmêtre, for what it's worth." But this isn't right; the process of embodiment does not consist just of showing us a fleeting glimpse of a mute body (and never frontal at that) plus a voice that supposedly belongs to it—leaving it up to the spectator to mentally assemble the separate elements. Real embodiment comes only with the simultaneous presentation of the visible body with the audible voice, a way for the body to swear "this is my voice" and for the voice to swear "this is my body." It must be a kind of marriage with a contract, consecrating the bonding of the voice to the habitat of the body, defusing and warding off the acousmetric forces. Which doesn't happen here.

2. *The scene on the landing.* The second moment of the mother's voice in *Psycho* occurs when Norman goes upstairs to his mother's bedroom to get her to a hiding place, since everyone is looking for her. The suspense in this scene hangs on nothing if not the prospect of de-acousmatizing the Acousmother.

At first the camera follows Norman from behind as it goes up the stairs with him. But when Norman enters the bedroom through the open door, the camera does not go in, because it has already separated from him and remains outside on the stairs, moving up all in the same shot in such a way that it ends up above the landing, looking over it from a bird's-eye perspective. It watches from there as Norman emerges from the room carrying his mother. In the preceding moments we've listened to an offscreen conversation from the bedroom, between Norman and his mother. Her voice is still haughty, but closer-up, no longer shouting, with no reverb, with a drier quality than before. This voice we are getting nearer to seems almost to be touching the frame from offscreen, causing us to expect, to fear, the de-acousmatization. The offscreen dialogue:

NORMAN: Now, mother, I'm going to bring something up—

MOTHER: I am sorry, my boy, but you do manage to look ludicrous when you give me orders.

NORMAN: Please, mother.

MOTHER: No, I will not hide in the fruit cellar. Ha! You think I'm fruity, huh? I'm staying right here. This is my room and no one will grab me out of it, least of all my big, bold son!

NORMAN: They'll come now, mother! He came after the girl, and now someone will come after him! Mother, please, it's just for a few days, just a few days so they won't find you.

MOTHER: Just for a few days? In that dark, dank fruit cellar? No! You hid me there once, boy, and you won't do it again, not ever again! Now get out! I told you to get out, boy!

NORMAN: I'll carry you, mother.

MOTHER: Norman, what do you think you're doing? Don't you touch me, don't! Norman! Put me down. Put me down, I can walk on my own—

With these last words Norman comes out of the room, but the camera has already assumed its bird's-eye perspective so that in this brief moment when he appears and begins down the stairs, and during which we hear the mother, we can only indistinctly see the body he is holding. Very rapidly, a fade to black ends this glimpse, accompanied by an aural fade to silence of the mother's voice on her last line. (It hardly needs saying that this choice to cut off the line of an important character at the end of a scene is rare in the sound cinema.)

We expect de-acousmatization to happen here; Hitchcock gives it to us only halfway, like a magician at once showing it and conjuring it into thin air. The disappearing act consists, of course, in using the extreme high-angle shot that makes it hard to see, and also in fading out before we've been able to see or hear much of anything—just at the moment when we'd hoped we could have both voice and body

145

together. As the scene ends the mother's voice remains in wait of a body to take her in.

This scene insistently harks back to the primal scene, in the words of the offscreen mother, with the terrifying double meaning of aggression and desire: "Don't touch me! Don't touch me!" This line suggests two bodies together, the sight of which is both anticipated and feared. And generally in fiction films, the terrorized attraction of going to see what one is hearing, often bears a close relation to the primal scene. The effect of the scene is reinforced by a "shuddering-cue," as Raymond Bellour puts it, created by the revelation at the end of the preceding scene that the mother is actually *dead and buried.* The sheriff's line cleverly displaces the question: "If the woman upstairs is Mrs. Bates, who is the woman buried in Greenlawn Cemetery?"

Few things in the cinema are as disturbing as this "disappearing act" on a de-acousmatization. Marguerite Duras creates a similar situation in *India Song.* The spectator is just about to see the synched speaking of the silent ghosts who move in the image and whose voices we've been hearing offscreen. This produces the particularly fascinating and morbid effect of *India Song,* which draws its power from *leaving something forever uncompleted.* Doubtless, *Son Nom de Venise,* in which Duras applies the same soundtrack to images empty of characters, answered a need to conjure the ghostly wanderings of *India Song* away by giving it symbolic closure—definitively forbidding the voices to enter onscreen.

In Hitchcock's scene, what is given is taken away in the same movement. What is lost is lost in the very mechanism of its apprehension, and all this happens within one shot. Hitchcock explains why:

> I didn't want to cut, when he carries her down, to a high shot because the audience would have been suspicious as to why the camera has suddenly jumped away. So I had a hanging camera follow Perkins up the stairs, and when he went into the room I continued going up without a cut. As the camera got

146

up on top of the door, the camera turned and looked back down the stairs again. Meanwhile, I had an argument take place between the son and his mother to distract the audience and take their minds off what the camera was doing. In this way the camera was above Perkins again as he carried his mother down and the public hadn't noticed a thing. It was rather exciting to use the camera to deceive the audience.[8]

Regarding the choice of this overhead camera position, Hitchcock explains it in connection with the scene of the murder of Arbogast: "If I'd shown her back, it might have looked as if I was deliberately concealing her face and the audience would have been leery. I used that high angle in order not to give the impression that I was trying to avoid showing her."[9]

Doubtless Hitchcock did not have to adopt such an elaborate strategy in order to maintain suspense. It seems to me that it's the very operation of belief that he tried to push to its limit, by applying a law of *montage interdit* or "forbidden montage" (whose rule is "don't cut"), which Bazin had considered a touchstone of the impression of reality in the cinema.

You might say that Hitchcock's words to sum up the audience's suspicions—"Why has the camera suddenly jumped away?"— recall *coitus interruptus*. Note that the scenes where Hitchcock refuses to cut, to edit, are often kissing scenes. For him, cutting such scenes into component shots would amount to breaking up the couple. "I think one can do a lot with love scenes," he says (cf. the very lengthy kissing shot in *Notorious*). During his conversation with Truffaut he tells the story of a strange love scene he never shot. From this rather smutty scene, let us merely report that it is again based on the disjunction between the dialogue and the situation. The situation involves words that diverge from what is seen, and by their very contrast, reinforce it. Equallyinstructive is the nature of a personal memory etched in his mind, which he recounts to explain his decision *not to cut*. Traveling in a French train, he said, he witnessed a young couple embracing by the

8. Truffaut, *Hitchcock*, pp. 208–210.
9. Ibid., p. 208.

147

wall of a factory. "The boy was urinating against the wall and the girl never let go of his arm. She'd look down at what he was doing, then look at the scenery around them, then back again at the boy. I felt this was true love at work."[10] Again we have a sort of *ménage à trois*, involving the two partners and Hitchcock's look from the train, returned by the girl. In all these scenes, the spectator's look is implicated as a third party with respect to the couple.

It happens that the no-cutting rule that Hitchcock has imposed on himself here was theorized by André Bazin in connection with an entirely different kind of scene: fights between man and beast. But isn't there something bestial in the image of the couple constituted by Norman and his mother? Bazin's text, published in 1953, explores the issue of verisimilitude in cinema, and what happens to the "reality effect" when a fight between man and beast is simulated by means of the artifices of editing. Bazin states that we simply won't believe the scene if the man and beast are shown in separate shots. We have to have at least one shot showing them together in order to believe. He cites Chaplin, who in *The Circus* is "truly in the lion's cage, and both are enclosed within the framework of the screen."[11] So his aesthetic is as follows: "When the essence of a scene demands the simultaneous presence of two or more factors in the action, montage is ruled out. It can reclaim its right to be used, however, whenever the import of the action no longer depends on physical contiguity."[12]

We could analyze the scene on the landing equally well along the Hitchcockian principle of "not breaking up the couple" or according to the Bazinian principle of "showing the man and beast together" (the living man and the murderous dead woman, here in a clinch). For whether it's a human couple or a man and animal, it amounts to the same thing for the primitive horror of sex.

For even as he shows us man and beast, or son and mother, or body and voice together, Hitchcock has to whisk them away. For the beast is a half human, the mother is a mummy, and the voice comes not from the mother's body (except by a sort of macabre ventriloquism), but from Norman as he plays both parts. It's as if the film

10. Ibid., p. 199.
11. Bazin, "The Virtues and Limitations of Montage," in *What is Cinema?* Hugh Gray, trans. (Berkeley: University of California Press, 1967), p. 52.
12. Ibid., p. 50.

were pinpointing the very essence of the unfilmable: the entwined couple, monstrous, the two-backed beast of the primal scene, the impossible couple of body and voice.

The scene on the landing is constructed so as to end up with the effect of voice and body lightly touching, brushing up against one another, approaching the limits of the "effet de réel," much more than in the convention of synchronization.[13] (Let us say in passing, if the voice that's totally liberated from bodies in Duras's films is often sublime, with other filmmakers the disembodied voice represents a system that's quickly exhausted. For even if the voice fastened to the body forms a conventional couple we might want to break up, *if it's removed far from the body, it can quickly get bored.*)[14] In *Psycho*, as in *India Song*, they brush up against each other at the end of a long asymptotic trajectory, but why is there something horrible in this touching—why does the wing of death seem also to brush the spectator?

3. *The holding cell.* The third moment of the mother's voice, as noted before, comes after Marion's sister Lila discovers the real mother is a mummy, and after the psychiatrist's monologue that meticulously analyzes the story and gives it a logical explanation that accounts for all the events of the film. So everything seems to be resolved. But when someone announces that the prisoner is feeling chilled and a policeman takes a blanket into the cell, the camera follows the policeman (as it had followed Norman up the stairs). The spectator still hopes to see the incestuous marriage between the mother's voice and Norman's body. Again, we first hear the mother's offscreen voice saying "thank you," before we enter the cell. But when we hear the voice over Norman's face—the mother's monologue—his mouth is closed, as if to suggest possession by spirits, or ventriloquism. Ultimately the voice has not found a body to own it and assign it a place—just as the burial of the mother did not take place according to correct custom since it was exhumed and stuffed. In order for the story to have closure, the corpse discovered in the cellar would have to be symbolically reburied. Instead, the very last

13. ["effet de réel": Chion is alluding to the Real in the Lacanian sense (the three registers of the Imaginary, Symbolic, and Real), that is, the encounter with the impossible. *Trans.*]

14. [Lacan associates sexual liberation with ennui. Chion here proposes a reading of the voice as something that can liberate itself from the body-as-prison. *Trans.*]

149

shot of the film is yet another image of unearthing, the dredging of Marion's car—her coffin—from the pond. Other allusions to burial or to its "opposite," taxidermy, indicate the prominence of this motif in *Psycho*. It's no surprise that the ghost's voice reigns over the final image, which consecrates the triumph of the acousmêtre. This is the same story as in *The Testament of Dr. Mabuse*, with which *Psycho* shares a number of similarities.

Both films revolve around a being who is hidden from us, and whose voice attests to his/her existence and power. In both, it is impossible to reunite the voice with a body that would orient it in space, in a body that isn't buried (Mabuse's dissected, dispersed body, the mother's stuffed body). Both films are concerned with the vocal possession of a man by an acousmêtre that's stronger than he (Baum by Mabuse, Norman by the mother). In both we find a shadow behind a backlit curtain, attesting to the presence of the Master, and in both a man who takes on the voice of his mother (Hofmeister in his madness when he tries to conjure away the horror, and Norman). Further, in both there is the intrusion of a woman into a forbidden space (Lily goes into the curtained room, and the similarly-named Lila, into the cellar). This intrusion leads to a revelation, in both cases of a non-human—no Mabuse, but a mechanical arrangement; no living mother, but a mummy. Finally, both plots end with the total identification of the weak character with the strong one, which seems to occur at the cost of permanent madness and incarceration: Baum with Mabuse, and Norman with his mother.

We know that Hitchcock saw Lang's film, but I don't believe that he consciously lifted the story's framework for his own, since it differs so much, in so many ways. It's simply that both films engage the same myth of the acousmêtre with the same rigor, the same desire to push at cinema's limits. *The Testament of Dr. Mabuse* as well as *Psycho* expose the very structure of sound film, based on an offscreen field inhabited by the voice, which is the inevitable corollary of the onscreen field. Finally, these two films also evoke the power to return the dead to life through sound and image. Both revolve around the illusion of sight and hearing, an illusion upon which the cinema is based, and in these films the cinema is drawn to its "impossibilities." The voice and the image can only appear as cut apart, they cannot consummate their reunion in a forever lost mythic unity. The talking film is but a jerry-rigged assemblage, and perhaps in this condition it finds its greatness. Instead of denying this rigging, it can choose it as its subject matter, taking that route, under the sign of the impossible, to the very heart of the effect of the Real.

Armin Jordan in *Parsifal*
(Hans-Jürgen Syberberg,
1982).

TEN THE CONFESSION

1   Words were uttered, but they have been lost or removed. What remains is an image of moving lips, of the body that utters. An unseen actor molds her diction to these moving lips and her voice is hitched to the image to take the place of the absent words. This is what is called *dubbing* (related terms: post-synchronization, looping, ADR). An actor may be dubbing her own lips, or the lips of another, but in any case there is *doubling*. This is why dubbing may produce disturbing effects of mismatching, where voices seem to waver around bodies (Fellini, Tati), or produce monsters and ghosts (*The Exorcist*). Sound loiters around the image like the voice around the body. What prevents it from being definitively fixed there is the words that have been lost or suppressed, the words of the original utterance that the image attests to. These words cannot be forgotten. Dubbing produces a palimpsest beneath which there runs a ghost-text. It is a *centrifugal* process, tending toward rupture and dispersion. It is proper to the sound film, since it was invented alongside the sound film.

Words were/are uttered by voices. Over these words, actors (whether or not they're the owners of these voices) make their bodies sing, speak, move. This time it is the body that molds itself precisely to the voice, the image that is constructed to match the sound. This is what is called *playback*, an age-old process. There can be "live playback" (puppet theater, opera, circus, ventriloquism), or time-delay playback (film, cartoons). In the cinema, playback was apparently in use by 1905, in the first experiments with talking and singing films. Playback is essentially *centripetal*, tending strongly toward concentration and tension. A grafting with respect to the original text, it presupposes the dropping of words that have been uttered, but those words pronounced during shooting are but a secondary text, the one that is built upon. With playback, the body tends to incorporate the voice, in aspiring to achieve an impossible unity.

TOP: Edith Clever in *Parsifal.*
BOTTOM: Günther Reich and
Louis Devos in *Moses and
Aaron* (Danièle Huillet and
Jean-Marie Straub, 1974).

Dubbing is generally used for *spoken* text, and playback for *sung* text; there are exceptions in both cases.

Playback, which became widespread with television, is often used to produce a sense of ubiquity. You film the body that mimes the voice (whether its own or not) anywhere you want and put the images together: on horseback then in a boat, in a bathtub and then on a stage—and it's the voice, this placeless entity, that guarantees continuity, provides *unity of place*. This is an amusing effect of playback, but a bit lightweight and so overused that it often gives way to a preference for the tension of "direct sound."

Playback and dubbing are procedures that inspire suspicion in cinema, because they're trick effects.

Then along comes Hans-Jürgen Syberberg, who after Straub, Bergman, and Losey, undertakes the fourth opera-film of the modern cinema (we won't speak of the numerous efforts that came before). His idea was to use actors in the image, rather than the original singers. What if these actors didn't pretend to be singing? He seems to roll this idea around in his head briefly, but finds himself chained to the logic of playback. If they don't pretend, it won't work, the body and the voice won't recognize each other. So all the characters will have to submit to the rules of lip-synch—but not shamefully, not hidden, on the contrary in the full glory of playback. Here Syberberg brings his camera close, closer than anyone before, to the deeply moving face of Armin Jordan lip-synching the voice of Wolfgang Schöne for the character of Amfortas. We see the dark cavern of the mouth, the monstrosity of lips in action, the strange beast of the tongue that moves from the depths of the throat, all to try to grasp the voice. And we are completely moved by it. Elsewhere, he withdraws from us (as we watch) the young man who served as Parsifal's body-on-loan, only to replace him *on screen* with a young woman who takes up where the other ostensibly left off the singing of tenor Reiner Goldberg; she continues to observe the ritual of synchronization even though she isn't "physically" credible, all to the horror or marvel of the spectator. Whatever the case, something amazing seems to be going on here. To top it all, in act III, the two bodies of the boy and the girl *both* conscientiously mime the one voice, standing side by side in the same shot.

Wagner might call this the "Erlösung" or redemption of playback, of its composite and underhanded nature. Why? Because here playback flaunts itself as such, by emphasizing the alterity of the body from the voice it tries to be attributed to.

Syberberg's film says that there is no Parsifal in the sense of a whole and unique being, this impossible conjuncture of compassion, knowledge, chastity, simplicity of soul (*"Durch Mitleid wissend, der reine Tor"*).[1] Rather, there are at least two beings who are like the two unjoinable halves that Plato speaks of in his *Symposium*. Syberberg's use of playback tells us also that there is no homogeneity of body and voice, none in any case that the cinema can show in a way that is *real* (this "cheating of direct sound," as Duras writes); there is only a *yearning* (German has a word for this, "Sehnen") for unity, and the cinema can show this yearning. It's even one of the things cinema is best at telling us about.

In dubbing, someone is hiding in order to stick his voice onto a body that has already acted for the camera. In playback there is someone before us whose entire effort is to attach his face and body to the voice we hear. We're witnessing a performance whose risks and failures become inscribed on the film. No emotion arises from dubbing as such. Since its work is unseen it produces only indirect effects, although they're occasionally beautiful. Playback is a source of a direct, even *physical* emotion. I'm thinking not only of Syberberg's film, but also of certain shots of Judy Garland, Bing Crosby, and Liza Minnelli in Hollywood musicals. Playback marshals the image in the effort to embody.

1. This formula defines in Wagner's opera the redeemer awaited by the Knights of the Grail. The idea is more or less: "By compassion gifted with knowledge, he is the chaste fool."

2   We must return to *The Jazz Singer*, officially the first talking film. In fact, this famous film has only one "talking" scene, which actually hadn't been planned as such and which was more or less improvised during shooting. Moreover, the film is only "singing" with

synch sound for about one-fourth of its running time. It remains essentially silent in its aesthetic, with intertitles and recorded or-chestral accompaniment for the rest of its three-quarters. But already it features, alongside the direct sound, the modest use of playback and even a bit of the Syberbergian procedure of *substituting one body with another*, in the scene where Jakie Rabinowitz (Al Jolson) goes to hear the religious melodies sung by a cantor, whose voice reminds him of his own father's. We see the image of the father take over that of the cantor and continue in playback over the same voice.

Elsewhere in the film, we get the reverse: two voices over the same body. When Al Jolson is supposedly performing the Kol Nidre at the synagogue, the film foregoes Jolson's own light and fluent voice, which we heard singing "jazz." He lip-synchs to the voice of a real cantor—but we are not supposed to know.

It's also in playback that the first sung scene in the film is done, when the young Jakie appears on a stage in a club. We see how awkwardly the young actor is miming the song that seems to have been recorded by an adult voice. So awkwardly, in fact, that it had to be shot from fifty feet away, and the filmmakers inserted many shots of the club audience in order to draw attention away from the obvious fact that the boy isn't really singing. It would take another fifty-five years to execute the camera movement up to a big closeup of the pseudo-singer's very throat to get the definitive admission that he's not the one singing, and more important, to raise to the level of a principle the fact that the cinematic body and voice are strangers to each other.

The subject of *The Jazz Singer* is an impossibility. It is impossible for Jakie/Jack to be at once a jazz singer to fulfill his life's dream, and the cantor in the synagogue in order not to lose his identity. It is impossible to occupy both the profane and sacred worlds at once, to hearken to the infinite love of the mother and the inexorable law of the father. This is all posited as a double-bind, an intractable dilemma, only to disappear ultimately into thin air. At the end it's as

157

Karin Krick and Michael
Kutter in *Parsifal*.

if Rabinowitz could at the same time, all in one evening, be both at the synagogue and at the theater. Today Syberberg says to us that this is impossible, the idea of one Parsifal who responds to all our expectations of him. But he shows this impossibility for what it is, by the "diachronic" doubling of Parsifal into two figures (briefly shown together at the end under the sign of utopianism) and by the "synchronic" doubling of persons in body and in voices. This act of showing impossibility can only be unique, and anyone trying to repeat this gesture after Syberberg tries it too late.

The impossibility common to *The Jazz Singer* and *Parsifal*, as films, is the fusion of body and voice, or what I have proposed to call the *integral anacousmêtre*.

3   Playback à la Syberberg thus takes up the process in reverse. When a body-lending, face-lending actor mimes the moving lips and body in lip-synch with the prerecorded voice, isn't this in order to make us believe that it is he? But when this body-lending actor is ostensibly designated as foreign to the voice attributed to him—either because physically the body doesn't go with the voice (a girl's face with a man's voice), or because two bodies are competing to "claim" the voice—what's the use of synchronization then? Let's drop this formality! This is what the sublime Edith Clever tried to do at first for her role, as we know, but that didn't work. We might think in fact that nothing tied the image to the voice any longer, aside from some vague convention or principle. But what becomes of synchronization if it is no longer supposed to conquer our belief? Is it merely there to impress us with the technical and physical prowess by which it synchs the actress to the singer's voice? No, not just that. It takes on an almost ritual meaning. It is an observance, it restates the words already spoken in order to re-actualize them. Through synchronization, the image tells the soundtrack, "stop floating around and come live within me." The body opens up to welcome the voice. This is the opposite of Bresson's strategy, where the dubbed voice filters out almost regretfully from the tight enclosure of the lips.

In playback, the body confesses to being the puppet brought to life by the voice. In *Parsifal*, everything begins with the puppet (think of the Prelude, and the awakening of the Flower-Girls). Elsewhere I have suggested the parallel between Orson Welles's work and the primary experience of puppet theater, where the child projects his own voice. Remember that among Welles's projects was a film to be shot entirely in playback over prerecorded voices. The fact that he never realized this project may well be due to the technical problems posed by synching to the unstable flow of speech (while the flow of song is, in western music at least, metronomic and thus easier to follow). In the films of Syberberg as well as Welles, there is this point of departure of the voice, which started out and always will be but a visitor in the house of the image.

Let us return to a moment of passing the torch in the middle of Syberberg's *Parsifal*. Parsifal One, the boy, has torn himself away from his mother's kiss; he begins to take on substance and humanity. But then Parsifal Two the girl arrives, places herself alongside him, and takes up "singing" earnestly where he left off, while Parsifal One fades out. With the latter, while his youth seemed a bit improbable as the source of the manly and vigorous tenor voice he carried, we could still believe that it was he. With Parsifal Two, the body knows it is only a temporary housing; it no longer hopes to fuse with the voice. From this comes its sadness, behind the cold and determined mask of Karen Krick. She must get through the score, accomplish what has been written.[2]

2. This essay appeared in *Cahiers du cinéma*, no. 338 (July–Aug., 1982) pp. 53–55.

This volume originally appeared in 1981, and one might question its relevance today. Do the films of the last fifteen to twenty years offer new cases, new aesthetic and theoretical challenges? I think so. Even though it was not the intent of *La Voix au cinéma* to chronicle a history of the voice from the cinema's beginnings to the present, I nevertheless think it appropriate now to offer to the reader of this edition several new ideas inspired by developments in recent films. This occasion also permits me to focus and reframe certain positions consciously or "unconsciously" taken in my book.

When *La Voix au cinéma* came out in France, a few readers commented that I was putting vastly disparate films into one undifferentiated basket—such as art films like Dreyer's *Ordet* and popular films like the thriller *When a Stranger Calls*. Believe me when I say that I hadn't noticed, and that I was harboring no particular hidden agenda. I find it natural not to draw cultural distinctions or hierarchies among films. How can we clearly distinguish "quality" films from "entertainment" films anyway, when films that in the '50s seemed the very height of gratuitous and frivolous entertainment (e.g., Hitchcock films like *North By Northwest*) are now considered works of art, and justly so? *The Testament of Dr. Mabuse*, one of the two films the book focuses on, was long regarded as a distraction devoid of significance; Lang's *M*, *Metropolis*, or *Fury* were considered more important since they carried a visibly social or political message. Numerous were those as well, upon the release of *Psycho*, who criticized the normally subtle and sophisticated Hitchcock for ostensibly being carried away by vulgar gothic effects of the horror genre. Time has shown the symbolic richness of both *Psycho* and *The Testament of Dr. Mabuse*, which had been judged minor works in contrast to their respective auteurs' "psychological" masterpieces.

I do not know if John Carpenter's *The Fog*, one of the genre films the book alludes to, will someday be considered a classic. But I do find a real poetry, subtlety, and innovativeness in this film, as well as relevance to the issue of the voice; all these qualities render it entirely worthy of being analyzed on the same plane as any other work. In the remarks that follow as well, I bring up many films not generally considered important since they're not inscribed into canonical film histories. If I insist on this point particularly with regard to American movies (which are underrepresented in the 1981 edition), it's because to my mind they seem to have been especially creative.

Three American films of the '70s mark big changes in the cinematic voice. First, *The Exorcist* contributed significantly to showing spectators how the cinematic voice is "stuck on" to the cinematic body. This grafting of heterogeneous elements can be seen as *The Exorcist*'s very subject. Audiences could stop thinking of the voice as a "natural" element oozing from the body on its own. The plot of *Singin' in the Rain* hinges on the notion that the natural voice of the actress played by Jean Hagen is vulgar and discordant with the star image she embodies on the silent screen. Enter the talkies, and the Debbie Reynolds character provides the voice allowing for the reconstitution of a harmonious being on the screen. Such films were thus based on the belief in the possibility of recreating a natural unity through dream, trick effects, or fantasy, and of finding the "right" voice for the "right" body. This belief disappears in the 1970s: there is no "natural" voice; every voice is a construction and forms a particular composite with the body. Each actor can take on different voices according to the demands of the role.

Dustin Hoffman might well be one of the first actors who manifest this vocal work. Think of his role as the little Italian-American in *Midnight Cowboy* (1969). But the real watershed for vocal composition or recreation comes in 1971 with Marlon Brando in *The Godfather*. Brando's hoarse, cracking, intimate voice makes you aware of its sound and timbre, as well as its fabricated nature. It's a voice that makes you listen consciously, and in the movie it conspicuously reorganizes all space around it. This effect was reinforced when, in what was one of the first great film sequels, *The Godfather, Part II*,

Robert de Niro played the role of the young Don Corleone. He developed a voice for the role that was consistent with the voice of his older character already played by Brando. As we know, the Godfather's voice would subsequently be pastiched and parodied ad infinitum in advertising, TV, and movies. It's a voice that belongs to the cinema, since it can exist only in vocal closeup.

This is not to say that no one had used the vocal closeup or the whispered voice in movies before. Recall the furtive, complicitous tone of Jimmy Stewart in *Rear Window*, and some of the voices used by Orson Welles in *Touch of Evil* or *The Trial* (where the director himself dubs several voices). But the '70s films changed the rules of the game, since they transformed diffuse undercurrents into marked effects, in somewhat the same way as Sergio Leone made the popular audience more conscious of the visual mechanisms of editing and mise-en-scène.

It is no accident that this change is linked to Italy—possibly owing to Italy's traditions of puppetry (where we're constantly aware that voices are grafted onto bodies, only temporarily on loan) and opera (where the relation between the sung voice and bodies seen from a distance also cannot be taken as natural). Already with Fellini, the voice is close up, insinuating, and we are conscious of our own experience of it. But perhaps the change came to the popular cinema from the fact that the heterogeneity of the voice and body has become much more consciously perceived.

In 1976 came George Lucas's *Star Wars*, the third film I see as very influential. *Star Wars* did not only contribute to the popularization of Dolby, through its spectacular audio and spatial effects. It was also striking in terms of its insistent use of masked characters, whose voices reach us like the voices of animated puppets. Think of C3PO, the talkative robot with an English butler's accent, and of the exquisitely bronzy voice of James Earl Jones, accompanied by those memorable breathing sounds in auditory closeup.

It is well known that *Star Wars* adapts a number of characters or figures from *The Wizard of Oz*. C3PO is a sci-fi version of the Tin Man, and the furry giant Chewbacca updates the Cowardly Lion. The little dog Toto is refigured in the diminutive chirping robot R2D2. The Wizard has become Darth Vader, the masked samurai. The scene where the dog Toto opens the curtain has a parallel in the third installment of the trilogy, *Return of the Jedi*, when the mortally wounded Darth Vader removes his disguise, and we see the face of a good man, disarmed, whose voice has lost its cavernous potency.

If I were to simplify as unhesitatingly as I did in first writing *La Voix au cinéma*, I'd say that in terms of developments in the cinematic voice, this kind of masked character constitutes a new sort of *ambulatory acousmêtre inside the image*, speaking into our ear from the center of the screen; we can sense that something has indeed evolved in the relation between sound and image.

Dolby helps to give a direct, close, and palpably physical presence to the voice, entirely changing the way we perceive it. More generally, it focuses finer attention on vocal texture, subtle variations of timbre, vibration of vocal cords, resonances. Multitrack sound helps to situate the voice in a more precise relation to other sounds that may be spread out in various directions in space (a phenomenon I discussed in *Audio-Vision: Sound on Screen*). Filmmakers can now bring sounds into play *with one another* to define cinematic space, whereas formerly their principal engagement of audiovisual space had to occur in the interplay between the low-fi monophonic soundtrack and the screen.

The screen is dispossessed. Sound may come from outside the screen. The transition from monophony to multitrack overhauls the rules of the game. The voice may be contained in a space that is no longer defined solely in visual terms, but also auditory ones. Its real positioning in a three-dimensional auditory space, in the middle of other sounds, takes away its imaginary place. The voice wishing to dominate must do so in a changed kind of space, which voices can no longer "contain" in the same way.

Everything that was only imaginary can now become real; voices can circulate around and beyond the screen, in orbit (the ghost voices in *Poltergeist*, space communications in numerous sci-fi films like *Alien*). Individual filmmakers don't necessarily have to make use of this real space where sounds circulate, but the perceptual expectations of today's spectator are more and more determined by it.

But also, in several respects, the screen is becoming the *mask* of the voice that speaks from its center, with a clear and strong timbre, as if amplified by the screen.

This phenomenon may be related to the predilection for radio in recent movies. Since *American Graffiti* (1973) in particular, radio has been showing up again and again as a subject. Think also of *Good Morning Vietnam* (1987, Barry Levinson), with the improvisations of disc-jockey Robin Williams, Woody Allen's *Radio Days*, Oliver Stone's *Talk Radio*, Spike Lee's *Do the Right Thing*, or Terry Gilliam's *The Fisher King* (not to mention TV's *Frasier* and *Northern Exposure*).

One must always view the relationship between technical possibilities and aesthetic and dramatic expression as a dialectic. The relation between the two is not unilateral. Quantitative technical changes (the possibility of expanding the vocal register, of making it possible simultaneously to clearly hear a dialogue, a voiceover narrator, and a song whose lyrics function like a subliminal commentary on the action—cf. Scorsese) also have unforeseen qualitative consequences: the voice doesn't necessarily sound "more," but "differently." It has a different intimacy. Paradoxically, Dolby and other current sound techniques increase the feeling of a silence surrounding the voice, in creating around it a different frame.

Before modern sound, every sound and every silence in a film was embedded in a continuous background tone that provided a sort of sonic continuum. Since Dolby increases dynamic contrast, it makes silence deeper, and from these silences the voice emerges differently. This might well account for the many "dreamed voices" on the threshold between silence and whispering: Mickey Rourke in *Rumble Fish* (Coppola, 1983), Kyle McLachlan in *Dune* (David Lynch, 1985), the veiled voice of Harvey Keitel in *Ulysses' Gaze* (Theo Angelopoulos, 1995).

Of course, we may find in a given film from the 1930s–1950s the utilization of intimate voices: in *Nightfall* (1956) by Jacques Tourneur, and above all in Marcel Carné's *Le Jour se lève* (1939). *Rear Window* is also, as I have noted, a film largely whispered, and James Stewart's voice works wonders in creating the feeling that we are there with the character.

But a sort of general poetic fog, a background noise still envelops the films of the '30s and '40s, while the sound of the '70s and '80s, because of technical evolution, becomes increasingly analytic. Each element is separate from the others, and the silence between sounds can become more palpable. In the same way that the visual format of CinemaScope passed from the stage of fullness to that of emptiness, and that it was discovered to be a way to emphasize *emptiness* in the image, as certain Japanese filmmakers admirably demonstrated, I think that today we are in the age when Dolby is discovering the beauty of silence around sounds, particularly around voices. Think of Kurosawa's *Dreams*, Kieslowski's *Double vie de Véronique* and *Blue*, and the later films of David Lynch such as *Wild at Heart* and *Lost Highway*. (Because of very loud and rhythmic passages of rock music, one forgets that the latter two films have many sequences in which auditory emptiness envelops confidences, and scenes where dialogue is slow and sparse.)

The more the cinema allows us to hear silence as such—silence in the sense of suspension of speech—the more value it gives to muteness. Think of two films directed by women, films centered on women who do not speak: *Children of a Lesser God* (Randa Haines, 1987), and *The Piano* (Jane Campion, 1993).

Children of a Lesser God, a beautiful drama based on a play by Mark Medoff, presents a very unsettling relationship between the voice and the body. The words of Marlee Matlin, expressed in sign language, are translated into speech (for the spectator's benefit, of course) by her lover William Hurt. Hurt's deep voice "envelops" the body and image of the woman, yet still leaves some mystery to her. One's eye looks to the image for the words uttered in gestural form.

168

Speech seems to have become a dance, more fluid, less discrete. Muteness, or rather the absence of a speaking voice in Marlee Matlin—an authentically deaf actor—is emphasized by the acoustic presence of her body; it is noteworthy that (thanks to Dolby) we hear the subtle sounds of clothing made by her graceful or vehement gestures. (In *The Piano*, the noises made by the mute Ada also play an important role, for they make the absence of her voice all the more striking). Sounds sketch out the body, so to speak. The irresistible desire to make the beloved woman speak ("say my name") is shown as a sort of impulse toward vocal rape.

It would also be interesting to consider the voice in relation to what it is not but which replaces it; I'm suggesting here that the acousmêtre of old sometimes takes the form now of a visible being on the screen. Take for example the classic film character of the ghost or invisible man. Today it is easy to make a film with a character who is supposedly invisible or inaudible to the other diegetic characters but not to us. This character has traits of the acousmêtre: he sees all, hears all, is ubiquitous, can go through walls, and can change form; but for us he is visible and opaque. Such are the guardian angels of Jerry Zucker's *Ghost* and Spielberg's *Always*. To be sure, these morality and fantasy tales owe much to Capra (*A Guy Named Joe, It's a Wonderful Life*), but they are doing something different.

Here we might pause to reflect on special effects or "tricks," which play an important role in many recent films, and to see what the voice has to do with them.

In one sense the voice is the first of special effects—the one requiring the fewest accessories, the least technology and money. A good actor or impressionist, in fact anyone with enough practice, can become capable of changing his voice and giving it all kinds of inflections and dimensions merely with the means nature has given him. The voice is itself the product of constant change in the organs and cavities that generate it. Strikingly, none of these "speaking parts" was designed specifically for the voice: mouth and lips, palate, tongue, teeth, and the airway for breathing. Even the so-called vocal

169

cords serve first to regulate respiration. So it can be said that there is no organ in the human body that is specific to phonation.

Two examples drawn from the history of monster movies illustrate the difference between the voice and the face in this respect: that of Jean Marais as the Beast in Jean Cocteau's *Beauty and the Beast* (1946), and John Hurt as John Merrick in David Lynch's *Elephant Man*. In both cases, a complex makeup job was necessary, executed by a master of the art—Arakelian for the Beast, and Rick Baker for Merrick. For the voice, on the other hand, the actors' talent and vocal technique sufficed, without the slightest technological aid.

We might imagine that for the infant, it must be frightening when there is a change in the voice of a familiar adult. Such changes or deformations might conjure up caricatural, monstrous, exaggerated faces in his imagination—like those seen in Tex Avery's cartoons.

So let me suggest that the cinema's recent predilection for deformed faces and bodies is a visual transposition of the terrifying impressions created during the first months of life by the disconcerting variability of vocal expression—thus a displacement of the heard onto the seen. For the very small human, parents and adults have an odor that remains constant, and a face that doesn't change shape much, but an unpredictable voice. Adult voices whisper, shout, laugh, cry, speak very close by or from afar, rise an octave, and in each case it's as if the adult becomes someone else. At the same time, for the adult spectator, a deformed voice has less immediate effect and spectacular power than a disfigured face. Maybe this is because the adult has understood that it's easier to alter the voice, and he gets his bearings from other cues—the body shape, the accent, tics or eccentricities of speech, clothing style . . .

All that we have been saying about the voice helps remind us that the history of altered voices in films differs profoundly from the history of altered bodies. If you examine cases in recent films, you notice that the most striking and memorable examples are not those in which someone invented a brand new vocal texture or timbre, since this deformation has been possible for a long time (including all the

170

possibilities of slow and fast motion already in use in cartoons of the '30s), but rather those in which a strong link has been created between the voice and the body, the voice and face. It's in this relationship that something can emerge, and not in the voice taken in isolation.

For example *The Exorcist* uses the very ordinary process of dubbing to make multiple voices—old woman, monster—come out of the "possessed" girl. Other effects thrown in are as old as the phonograph, such as "backwards" sound and "slow motion." The whole thing takes on its horrific effect because of the *relationship*, the comparison the viewer makes between the visible body and the voice.

To make his E.T. speak, Spielberg used several voices, including an elderly woman whose voice was scarred by years of alcohol and tobacco, which gave her an inimitable hoarseness. Life, not technology, had done the work on this voice. What makes the film tick is the way it marries the extraterrestrial's unique form, his disproportionate and refractile neck and his unique gestures, to the voice that is dubbed in. This goes back to very old forms of theater where the voice and body are dissociated at first—notably the ancient art of puppetry, to which the cinema owes a great deal.

So a considerable number of recent movies, not only fantasy films, have focused not so much on altering voices (an old technique, so nothing startling or innovative there) as on discovering new relationships—shocking, terrifying, or picturesque—between voice and body. We find examples ranging from comedy-fantasies about sex inversion, where a woman speaks with a male voice and vice versa (e.g. the French film *Rendez-moi ma peau*, by Patrick Schulmann), or the Brechtian musical *Pennies from Heaven*, where Steve Martin breaks into song dubbed with a woman's voice, to comedies like the *Look Who's Talking* series, in which a baby's "thoughts" and impressions are communicated to us through an adult voice adeptly timed to match the infant's expressions; the voice is "stuck on" to the image. In the original film, the baby's inner voice is that of Bruce Willis, and in the French dub, it's the actor Daniel Auteuil.

171

It can be said that such a case is not new. For example, as early as 1936, Sacha Guitry, in *Story of a Cheat*, used his own voice to dub all the characters in his film. He thereby assumed the role of the puppet master, as Orson Welles has also done. But the difference is that today filmmakers go much farther in the alteration of bodies, which can engender entirely new possibilities in the relation between body and voice.

Let us add that today there exists a very influential new audiovisual form, the music video, which has opened the doors to infinite possibilities in representing relations between a voice and its source. It's based on playback, a process that even predates the cinema (it hails from the tradition of puppet theater). From the extreme close-up of lips, implacably accompanying the song in perfect synch, to the movement of objects or other visual forms synched to the articulation of a text (as in certain Peter Gabriel videos), not to mention all the possible relationships between the image of a mouth or some other movement articulated in the image, and a sung text on the soundtrack, the music video has been a laboratory, a place to explore in truly interesting ways the relations between voice and image. The cinema has benefited from it. For example it's probably thanks to the precedents set by music video that David Cronenberg, in his screen version of William Burroughs' *Naked Lunch*, found the audacity to engage his protagonist in a dialogue with a talking typewriter (which talks not through a "mouth" but through a kind of anal sphincter that reshapes itself obscenely as if to form the syllables being uttered). These are experiments in which, owing to the psycho-physiological phenomenon which in my work I have called synchresis, it can be seen that the voice and human speech are synchronizable with just about anything that moves.

The work that especially American actors devote to vocal accents and timbres also allows them to reassert their identity as actors, to show that they are not just blank canvases for makeup, but that they can reinvent and master their craft through technique, the body, and the voice.

172

The most spectacular impact of this work can be heard in voices of Anglo-Saxon actors playing invalids, handicapped characters, autistic people, or monsters: John Hurt in *Elephant Man*, Dustin Hoffman in *Rain Man*, Daniel Day Lewis in *My Left Foot*. Also noteworthy is their mastery of accents: Geena Davis and Susan Sarandon's southwest accents in *Thelma and Louise*, De Niro's southern accent in *Cape Fear*, Meryl Streep's many accents including Polish in *Sophie's Choice* and Australian in *A Cry in the Dark*, and so on.

Epilogue:
Cinema's Voices of
the '80s and '90s

But voicework does not stop with the acquisition of an accent. There is timbre, the way of creating a voice that's hoarser, more metallic, more full-throated, more sonorous, or less harmonically rich. Compare, if you will, two roughly contemporaneous Dustin Hoffman movies. In Barry Levinson's *Rain Man*, he has a metallic and nasal voice and in Stephen Frears' *Hero* it's coarser. If you listen to both films without the picture, it is quite difficult to identify both voices as coming from the same actor.

In France hardly any actors modify their voices, their way of speaking, or their accent for new roles. Daniel Auteuil is one of the very few to do so convincingly.

The consequence is that again, the audience becomes aware of the voice as an entity distinct from the body, even when it comes from the very center of the image. There has been a change since the 1950s in that the viewer cannot predict what voice De Niro or Streep might have in the newest film.

Another consequence of this voicework is that when American films are dubbed into French today, there is no longer the same dubbing-actor's voice used for each film of a star (for example, an actor named Roger Rudel always used to speak the voice of Kirk Douglas). The popular audience—those who watch dubbed prints of American films—thus do not always hear the same French actor's voice with a given American actor, whether Michael Douglas or Julia Roberts. The French viewer then becomes much more aware of dubbing as a practice. Only for movie stars in the classic sense—stars who always play themselves, like Arnold Schwarzenegger or Sean

Connery—do French spectators get to hear the same dubbing voice from film to film.

The voice is ceasing to be identified with a specific face. It appears much less stable, identified, hence fetishizable. This general realization that the voice is radically other than the body that adopts it (or that it adopts) for the duration of a film seems to me to be one of the most significant phenomena in the recent development of the cinema, television, and audiovisual media in general.

INDEX